ON WRITING AND WORLDBUILDING
Volume II

Timothy Hickson

Cover illustration by Chris Drake

First ebook edition published in 2021
ISBN: 978-0-473-59133-5

PREFACE

I remember the distinct feeling I had when I released 'On Writing: Hard Magic Systems' on the 8th of February 2018. That I had found something of value. Not merely financially, in the sense that you create something people willingly consume, but in that deeply personal way where you feel you contribute something to the world worth remembering. I don't mean to overstate what that video was—after all, it was just a thirteen-minute-long video that I wrote in under a week—but it marked a sharp pivot in my career towards education. I remember telling my partner very explicitly that I did not expect the video to get more than 10,000 views online. It was a pretty niche topic, and it was certainly outside my usual wheelhouse. You can imagine my shock when it reached over 200,000 views in its first few days.

Making educational content freely available to people has been a truly fulfilling experience for me in a way that the videos I was making before were not. That I was helping people improve their craft and follow their passion while also discussing stories I loved. I have always approached writing from that perspective of a reader, wanting to study why these stories have stuck with me. An exercise in sharing my findings more than telling other people how to write. It was part of me learning to do that myself. I have always loved studying why stories work—structure, pace, character, and all—and it was just an extension of that. Put a chain of words in the right order and you can make someone cry. Stories are the closest thing we have to magic.

Unavoidably, the line between studying stories like this and teaching people how to write is a blurry one. Teachers have to do both. While I don't see myself as writing from a position of authority, but as a dedicated reader and writer, I know some people have come to see me that way. It's both deeply validating and terrifying that people would trust my thoughts and ramblings as much as they do. The highest compliments I've received have been from teachers telling me they use my videos in their classes, assigning them for homework or as extra materials. Validating because it makes me feel like I am doing something right, and terrifying because I'm not sure I've earned that.

The Dunning-Kruger Effect is a well-known cognitive bias, and while it's more truly applied to large groups of people, it's hard not to apply it to yourself: that when you know little, you think you know a lot, when you know a fair bit, you will doubt yourself entirely, till eventually you do know a lot and you reach a plateau of moderate self-confidence. The paradox of the Dunning-Kruger Effect is that I cannot know where I fall on it. It's a lot easier to spot in other people than myself. People who find what I make helpful impress on me that I must know a lot, that I must be a skilled writer and worldbuilder, but given only I know how much I struggle, part of me believes that must be a lie—that believing it would be the peak that comes with the ignorance. At the same time, does my awareness of that mean that I am in fact a slowly coming to terms with being at least a little knowledgeable—that plateau of self-confidence?

I don't know. I certainly don't feel confident all the time, but I'm not constantly in self-doubt either. The nature of being an online personality is the constant juxtaposition of praise and criticism, and it warps your ability to judge yourself. Even after the overwhelming and unexpected success of *Volume I* and having others enjoy my writing, I find myself questioning whether I have earned or deserve the right to put out this book.

All I know is that some people find my discussions helpful, that I enjoy sharing them, and that my work has made some measure of difference in the writing journeys of others. I'm thankful I have had the opportunity to do that, and I need to focus on that rather than trying to pin down exactly how good I am at what I do. That way lies madness.

My life has changed a lot over the last two years, largely thanks to Alex Cuenin—my video editor. Alex, you are not only a joy to work with but a great man and good friend. You helped bring this series to life, but you also took an immense weight off my shoulders that has allowed me the time to write and submit stories to magazines, finish my fiction book, and work on things other than the channel. Thank you, Alex.

I want *On Writing and Worldbuilding: Volume II* to be a discussion you feel you can be party to. I have always steered away from the word 'should' because there are no writing rules; there are only things that are more satisfying to the average reader or things that might make a book more likely to be published. For every rule, there are ten exceptions, and for every ten exceptions, there is a masterstroke of genius writing. *Volume II* is a codified version of the online series with more detail, better and deeper examples, and thousands more words of analysis, and I hope it serves as a valuable educational resource that offers questions and points you may not have considered before in your own writing.

Here's hoping *Volume II* helps you in some small way.

Stay nerdy,

Tim

ON WRITING

WRITING FIGHT SCENES

Without Fail by Lee Child
The Poppy War by RF Kuang
Dark Matter by Blake Crouch
Harry Potter and the Order of the Phoenix by JK Rowling
Leviathan Wakes by James SA Corey
A Game of Thrones by GRR Martin
Skyward by Brandon Sanderson
The Hunger by Alma Katsu
The Girl with the Dragon Tattoo by Stieg Larsson
Harry Potter and the Deathly Hallows by JK Rowling
A Storm of Swords by GRR Martin
The Shining by Stephen King
The Great Hunt by Robert Jordan
Dune by Frank Herbert
Avatar: The Last Airbender by Mike DiMartino and Bryan Konietzko
Structuring Your Novel by KM Weiland
The Return of the King by JRR Tolkien
Pirates of the Caribbean: Dead Man's Chest directed by Gore Verbinski
Star Wars: A New Hope directed by George Lucas

It is no secret that fight scenes are hard to write, but we can break them down into two dimensions:

1. Macro → The broader structure and their place in the narrative.
2. Micro → The word-by-word and sentence-by-sentence flow of a fight scene.

There is already a lot of advice out there about how to manage the macro of a fight scene because similar rules apply to television and film, while extraordinarily little is dedicated to the micro. This chapter will first address the micro in detail before moving onto the macro.

Long versus short sentences

The first piece of advice many writers find when looking into writing fight scenes is that you should write shorter sentences, and it is true that some authors do use shorter sentences to better reflect the quick back-and-forth of a fight. Author of the *Jack Reacher* series, Lee Child, commonly shortens his sentences to never let a moment linger. Consider the following excerpt from *Without Fail*:

> Bismarck smiled. Tightened his finger. His knuckle shone white. He squeezed the trigger. There was a dull click. Reacher came out with his ceramic knife already open and brushed it sideways across the guy's forehead. Then he caught the Beretta's barrel in his left hand and jerked it up and jerked it down full force across his knee and shattered the guy's forearm. Pushed him away and spun round. Neagley had hardly moved. But the guy from the garage video was inert in the snow by her feet. He was bleeding from both ears.

These are not even complete sentences. 'Tightened his finger' lacks the grammatical subject 'he', as if complete thoughts are not possible in a tense moment like this. It creates the impression of urgency, more clearly mimicking our instinctual thought patterns in moments of tension. RF Kuang employs a similar technique in *The Poppy War* where shorter sentences reflect the brutal and sharp movements of the martial arts.

Unlike Venka, Nezha could absorb losses and continue. She bruised him once or twice. He adapted and hit her back. And his blows hurt. They were two minutes in.

... She was here to win. Exploding Dragon. Crouching Tiger. Extended Crane.

The next time she threw a punch he grabbed her arm and pulled her in close. Her breath hitched. He raked his nails across her face and down to her collarbone... Nezha had drawn blood.

... She dodged the first one. He swung his fist back in reverse and caught her with a backhand that left her gasping. The lower half of her face went numb.

He'd slapped her.

He'd *slapped* her.

... She couldn't breathe. Black tinged the edges of her vision—black, and then scarlet. An awful rage filled her, consumed her thoughts entirely. She needed revenge like she needed to breathe. She wanted Nezha to hurt. She wanted Nezha punished.

... No—pain led to success.

He struck her face once, twice, thrice.

These shorter sentences usually focus on a strong verb without many adjectives or other framing—'He *struck* her face once, twice, thrice'. The prose itself is very restrained, even minimalistic. The place of short sentences is well-defined, and it is worth taking note.

However, not only do these fight scenes also have a lot of long sentences as well, but a large enough share of fight scenes do not shorten their sentences for you to not take this as universal advice. It can even be advantageous to have longer sentences.

This is because writing a successful fight scene is less about sentence length and more about how the individual beats of a fight scene tend to be short. Consider this sentence in Blake Crouch's *Dark Matter*:

> I *slam* into the hardwood floor, the back of my head *hitting* so hard I see bursts of light, and then *he's on top of me*, blood dripping off his ruined face, one hand *squeezing* my throat.

Here, there are four distinct beats that happen in quick succession: slam, hitting, is on top of, squeezing—italicised for emphasis. There are far more verb beats than your average sentence, which usually only have one or two, and that each of these are short gives the feeling of fast-paced tension. Placing these actions in the same sentence can make it feel even faster because there is no full stop between them. No breath allowed.

Compare this with JK Rowling's wording in the fight between Dumbledore and Voldemort in *Harry Potter and the Order of the Phoenix*:

> Dumbledore *brandished* his wand in one, long, fluid movement—the snake, which had been an instant from *sinking* its fangs into him, *flew* high into the air and *vanished* in a wisp of dark smoke; the water in the pool *rose* up and *covered* Voldemort like a cocoon of molten glass...

Once again, speed and tension is not about sentence length. It is about how long an action beat takes: brandishing, sinking, flew, vanished, rose, and covered all happen in the same sentence—italicised for emphasis. A hell of a lot happens in this sentence, but each beat is just a handful of words. It is worth noting that action beats in here do not have the same sharpness that they do in *The Poppy War*. Where in *Harry Potter* each beat flows into the next, in *The Poppy War* each one feels deeply consequential on its own. Both, however, feel fast-paced.

Let your sentences be short and long, whichever fits your style. A chain of strong verbs can allow the reader to follow the fight beats as fast as they would take to happen. The sentence from *Harry Potter and the Order of the Phoenix* actually takes less time to say than the film does to show the same things happening.

<u>Cause and effect</u>

Having a series of verbs in quick succession does not an interesting fight make. Writing, 'Marwyn kicked his opponent, then thrust his fist into a punch, dodged left and cut up with his elbow into his enemy's jaw' is a sentence of verbs in quick succession, but it is neither interesting nor easy to follow. What you will notice about good fight scenes is that whether using short or long sentences, there is a strong feeling of cause and effect moving from one verb to the other. Take this passage from James SA Corey's *Leviathan Wakes*:

> Holden *shook* violently in his restraints and then *slapped* back into his chair as Alex took the Roci through a series of sudden manoeuvres and then *slammed* down the throttle to *evade* the last of the PDC fire.

Shook, slapped, slammed, and evade — italicised for emphasis. Each of these four beats' verbs arrive in quick succession, have a strong consequential relationship to the previous one, and then cause the one that follows. Holden shakes and slaps back into his chair because they are accelerating and evading, which are understandably rocky experiences.

This gives the reader a sense of chronology on a sentence-by-sentence basis. We can contrast this with our bad example from before — 'Marwyn kicked his opponent, then thrust his fist into a punch, dodged left and cut up with his elbow into his enemy's jaw' — which lacks any feeling of causation. Each movement feels ultimately pointless on its own because it has no bearing on the actions that follow. One test for this is asking if you are able to put your action beats in any order without it changing the flow of your fight scene. If you can, then it potentially lacks that cause-to-consequence flow.

We could perhaps improve our line from before by applying these lessons: 'Marwyn kicked the man to the dirt and pounced on him, driving a fist into his chest. The man scrabbled beneath him, forcing Marwyn to dodge his wild thrashing before he cut his elbow up into the man's jaw. He fell limp, strings cut.'

But in framing your cause-and-effect verb chains, there are patterns that a lot of writers use. A common one is the react-pause-act trio.

Consider this fight in GRR Martin's *A Game of Thrones*:

> And it must be said of Ser Vardis Egen that he was true to his lady's command, even to the last. One moment he was reeling backward, half-crouched behind his scarred shield; the next he charged. The sudden bull rush caught Bronn off balance.

The fight is centred around that second sentence. He reacts: reeling—he pauses: crouched—and he acts: charged. Likewise in Brandon Sanderson's *Skyward* when Spensa is being chased through the air by the enemy:

> I cut my acclivity ring, spun on my axis, then overburned right back downward.

React: cut—pause: spun—act: overburned downward. These patterns maintain that sense of cause and effect while also giving variety of pacing to the fight scene. The react-pause-act framework means the character is not doing the same thing over and over in different words. Instead of attacking, attacking, and attacking, they are changing tactics, considering surroundings, and being responsive, forced to take account of their last action.

We can see a second pattern in Blake Crouch's *Dark Matter*—the goal-conflict-disaster:

> Grabbing his head, I bring my knee back for another blow, but he sweeps my left leg out from under me. I slam into the hardwood floor.

Goal: grabbing—conflict: bring—disaster: sweep. This simple and fast-paced sentence model serves a different purpose. React-pause-act gives a sense of moving towards a goal, while goal-conflict-disaster moves a character further away from their objective. Using these two structures in tandem can give a compelling rhythm to a fight scene, shifting what is at stake moment to moment and carrying the reader along with the action. A back and forth as well as a cause to effect.

Though not in a single sentence, this scene from Sanderson's *Skyward* links these two patterns together:

> I got in close and speared [goal] the Krell ship with my light-lance. Then I turned, pulling [conflict] the Krell ship out of line with Bog. The cockpit trembled around me… sending [disaster] us both into a frantic out-of-control spin… I cut [react] my acclivity ring, spun [pause] on my axis, then overburned [act] right back downward.

Even so, do not think of these as rigid rules, but what they are: patterns and suggestions. Be creative in your sentence length and the number of beats you have, and remember that the cause-and-effect relationship is more important for clarity and rhythm. Variety in sentence structure is often helpful. It makes long passages easier to digest and keeps your prose interesting.

<u>Where should you give detail in a fight scene?</u>

While the cause-and-effect structure and those verb patterns will help, those alone do not make a well-paced fight scene. You do not need to write every moment of a fight scene in equal detail. Let us consider three main types of moments that tend to be described in depth.

The first is when there is a shift in the balance of power. Consider this fight in Alma Katsu's *The Hunger*:

> Before Stanton could pull his gun from its holster, the man tackled [1] him, knocking him to the ground. The whirling sand obscured details and made Stanton feel as though he were wrestling a faceless phantasm — one, however, who reeked of whiskey. Stanton managed to jerk aside when the man plunged a fist toward his face, and heard a knife blade strike [2] loose sand beside him.
>
> They rolled over and over in the sand, scrabbling for advantage, fighting not just each other but the wind, a giant hand hurling them through the dark… He caught [3] the man good in the ribs, though, and heard him cry out, and then Stanton was sure he recognised the voice. Lewis Keseberg.

There are three distinctly described moments in this fight here, each marked out [1], [2], and [3] in the text. The first is the inciting incident of the fight, where the balance of power shifts against Stanton as the man knocks him to the ground. In the second, a knife is introduced, raising the stakes, and shifting the balance further against him. He is not just pinned down but at risk of death. Finally, in the third, Stanton gains the upper hand by jabbing the man in the ribs and learning who it truly is.

An equally important phrase here is how Katsu describes the bulk of the fight: 'They rolled over and over in the sand, scrabbling for advantage.' Here, nothing specific is described, but the reader gets the idea of what is happening: two men wrestling over a knife in the dirt. The reason that nothing is described though is there is no shift in the balance of power. Describing this in detail would give specification without much purpose. It would neither move the fight forward nor change our relationship with the tension in this scene.

However, some fight scenes are not based around struggles for power but non-combat goals. In *The Girl with the Dragon Tattoo* by Stieg Larsson, Salander goes against a serial killer to free her friend Blomkvist, who is slowly suffocating. It is a race against time to free him. Because of this, Larsson describes in detail the moments where she gets closer or further away from that goal as well as the shifts in power—though there are not many.

It is worth considering where the reader will derive tension from during a fight scene. Is it simply from whether a character will make it out, or do they have another goal in mind? It is common in horror stories for one party to be entirely outmatched, and so a lot of the tension surrounds whether they will be able to reach a weapon or escape instead.

The second type of moment you might add more detail is when something important about a character is revealed or advanced. Let us return to *The Poppy War* and take a closer look at which moments get more detail:

> The next time Nezha lunged at her she pulled him to the floor with her. They rolled around in the dirt, each attempting to pin the other and failing.
>
> He punched madly in the air, flinging blows haphazardly at her face.
>
> She dodged the first one. He swung his fist back in reverse and caught her with a backhand that left her gasping. The lower half of her face went numb.
>
> He'd slapped her.
>
> He'd *slapped* her.
>
> A kick she could take. A knife hand strike she could absorb. But that slap had a savage intimacy.

Like in *The Hunger*, the moments of the fight where there are no major shifts in power are generalised: 'They rolled around in the dirt, each attempting to pin the other and failing'. However, the moment where Nezha slaps Rin is given particular attention. Rin grew up socially isolated and repeatedly beaten down, making this slap personally humiliating and degrading, and it motivates her to fight differently from then on. It plays into her arc, her strengths, and her flaws in a way that other beats do not. If there are moments where your characters are personally challenged or they take actions that indicate growth or failure, then describe them in more detail.

Lastly, you might linger for moments of narrative importance—things that you as the author want the character or reader to reflect on. Take the final duel between Harry Potter and Voldemort in *Harry Potter and the Deathly Hallows*:

> The bang was like a cannon blast, and the golden flames that erupted between them, at the dead centre of the circle they had been treading, marked the point where the spells collided. Harry saw Voldemort's green jet meet his own spell, saw the Elder Wand fly high, dark against the sunrise, spinning across the enchanted ceiling like the head of Nagini, spinning through the air toward the master it would not kill, who had come to take full possession of it at last. And Harry, with the unerring skill of the Seeker, caught the wand in his free hand as Voldemort fell backward, arms splayed, the slit pupils of the scarlet eyes rolling upward. Tom Riddle hit the floor with a mundane finality, his body feeble and shrunken, the white hands empty, the snakelike face vacant and unknowing. Voldemort was dead, killed by his own rebounding curse, and Harry stood with two wands in his hand, staring down at his enemy's shell.

This single moment is described in lengthy detail to allow the reader to feel the cathartic release of Voldemort's final defeat.

This moment takes place over just a couple of seconds, if that, and yet Rowling stretches it to give it a grandeur it would not otherwise have.

In discussing writing fight scenes, author Brandon Sanderson said, 'You are not writing a screenplay... If you describe [a blow-by-blow fight scene] in a book, no matter how well you describe it, it's going to be boring... Play to the strengths of [the novel] medium.'

He is right. Arguably the greatest strength of a novel is the reader's imagination. This is why generalised descriptions like 'they tussled on the ground for half a minute' work; the reader will easily better imagine it than you could describe it. It evokes a struggle without forcing you to detail it.

But I want to discuss two tools you can use to best utilise the reader's imagination for your benefit. Sebastien de Castell, author of *Traitor's Blade*, wrote on the importance of '[showing the reader] early on in the fight how each weapon moves through space—make them vivid and visceral... then you're free to focus on the character's actions and reactions.' This helps establish the feel and flow of the fight from the start—the back and forth.

One example of this is in GRR Martin's *A Storm of Swords* when Prince Oberyn took on the Mountain, Gregor Clegane:

> Oberyn's long spear jabbed, but Ser Gregor took the point on his shield, shoved it aside, and bulled back at the prince, his great sword flashing. The Dornishman spun away untouched.

This opening phrase establishes Oberyn as quick and darting, akin to a viper, and Ser Gregor as a mountain of a man with slow but brutal swings. It is because of this opening to the fight that more generalised statements later work. We already know how they move, the pace, and the types of attacks they deal and avoid. Show the way the people and weapons move and how the environment changes early on, and you can allow the reader to do the rest of the work for you.

Secondly, these generalised statements are also where more creative language comes in useful:

> They wrestled in the dust and blood… the Mountain had wrapped one huge arm around the prince, drawing him tight against his chest, like a lover.

These focus on giving a sensation to the fight rather than high-paced clarity, but during these more generalised moments, clarity becomes less important. You do not need those verb chains with these generalised statements. If you are looking for where to show off your unmatched metaphorical writing in a fight scene, it is here.

<u>Making it easy to follow</u>

More than usual scenes, fight scenes rely on the reader's understanding of space. Where characters are, what is around them, and their physical options for movement and action. Science fiction writer Rob Wells summarised this in saying:

> 'One of the biggest mistakes is we forget we are not a visual medium… We don't know what the room looks like, we don't know where the chairs are, so when a character picks one up [to fight] it can come out of nowhere. You need to set us up with the setting.'[1]

When talking about using space in this way, we need to talk about the Department of Mysteries in *Harry Potter and the*

---

[1] Brandon Sanderson, Dan Wells, Howard Taylor, Rob Wells "Fight Scenes" (podcast, 1 March 2009) Writing Excuses <writingexcuses.com>

Order of the Phoenix. Rowling writes intentionally to establish the space before the fight even begins, giving the reader a clear idea of how to visualise the fight when it happens later. Some authors fall into the trap of describing the space during the fight, slowing the pacing immensely and making it seem convenient when cover or escapes appear, but instead, Rowling writes so every spatial element that returns during the fight itself is set up pages prior:

> … he saw clocks gleaming from every surface, large and small… hanging in spaces between bookcases or standing on desks ranging the length of the room.

She then later returns to these spatial objects when she writes:

> A jet of red light hit the nearest Death Eater, he fell backward into a grandfather clock… Hermione [had] crawled under the desk to get a better aim.

Both the fragile clocks and the desks mentioned in the first description return in the fight scene as complicating factors, making it more interesting and keeping it easy to visualise by using these pre-established set pieces. Rowling does this repeatedly. All of this means she can focus on character and emotions during the fight because no words are wasted on setting the scene.

The use of space in a fight scene is like a series of Chekhov's guns: if you tell the reader there is a cliff nearby, there is an inherent fear and even expectation that someone will fall down it later on. If you mention a gun, then people almost expect it to come out in a fight later on. A fight is only as good as its build-up, and introducing those spatial elements beforehand creates an expectation and tension for the reader and characters, especially if you highlight obstacles like there being only one way out of a room. Fundamentally, if your environment is going to affect the way characters fight, then establishing it beforehand is helpful.

Because of this, a useful tool for planning fight scenes is blocking. This is a theatre term describing mapping out the movements of characters on a stage in broad strokes before the actors give it a shot. Rather than describing the characters' actions in a vacuum, visualise them in the space beforehand — what would they notice and use?

This can become more difficult when writing from a limited perspective — either first person or even third person limited, especially if a host of characters are involved in the fight. It can seem impossible that a single character would keep track of everyone. Again, *The Order of the Phoenix* manages this in a curious way.

Sirius' death is the single most important beat in this fight scene, but it is written from the perspective of a single character: Harry. Yet, it is Rowling's use of space that allows the story to naturally build to this moment, even in the chaos of numerous characters. Rowling regularly reminds the reader where characters are — reminding us where Sirius is four times leading up to his death:

> [Sirius was] now raining spells down upon them as [he] jumped from step to step toward the sunken floor.

> … through watering eyes [Harry] saw Sirius duelling with a Death Eater some ten feet away.

> Sirius yelled, dashing to meet Bellatrix…

> [Harry] saw Malfoy smash into the dais on which Sirius and Bellatrix were now duelling.

> Sirius had only just fallen through the archway.

The reader does not follow the other characters nearly as closely, but we do not need to. Their actions are largely inconsequential in the arc of the fight scene. We still get references to what they are doing during the fight, especially when they play a role in the balance of power shifting, but Rowling only carefully tracks the spatial journeys of characters who play crucial roles: Harry, Malfoy, Bellatrix, and Sirius. Because of this, Sirius' death atop the dais does not take us by surprise. We know where he is, how he got there, how far Harry is from him, and who did it. There is a clear arc to the scene without being obvious that it is leading up to Sirius' death.

Even if you are writing from a single perspective, give regular reminders to the reader where characters who play crucial roles in the fight scene story beats are.

<u>Word choice</u>

Sentence structure and pacing are one thing, but word choice is where you can craft the tone and feel of a fight scene. It is how you describe pain and the consequences to every blow. In Stephen King's novel *The Shining*, he repeatedly attaches visceral bodily descriptors to his fights that forge the dark tone of the scene:

> The mallet came down again with whistling, deadly velocity and buried itself in her soft stomach… Agony exploded on her right side as the mallet took her just below the line of her breasts, breaking two ribs… The mallet came down [and] landed just below her kneecap… She jerked her head away from it and it [scraped] away the flesh from her ear.

The Girl with the Dragon Tattoo employs a similar technique:

> The iron… hit Martin on the collarbone near his
> shoulder. The blow had a terrible force, and
> Blomkvist heard something snap.

Both authors deliberately use specific bodily descriptions to remind the reader how fragile we are, making it feel brutal, uncomfortable, and bloody. There is a lot more emphasis on avoiding blows because every blow that lands does so with serious consequence. Our heroes are not made of rubber. Death is constantly on the horizon, and the prose keeps reminding you.

We can contrast this with some more light-hearted fiction in Robert Jordan's *The Great Hunt*:

> Without the void, he was always half a heartbeat
> behind. The tip of Turak's heavy sword made a
> stinging trench just under his left eye. A flap of coat
> sleeve hung away from his shoulder, the darker for
> being wet… The River Undercuts the Bank. He
> dropped to one knee, blade slashing across.

The descriptors here for pain are far more generalised compared to Larsson and King. Characters are hit, but it is not usually devastating, and it reads without the same emphasis on gruesome bodily descriptors. Jordan's writing does not linger on the consequences of the fight. The focus is not nearly as much on avoidance. This is a tonal choice that makes it less gritty, more interested in spectacle and light-hearted. This is a technique employed by fiction aimed at younger audiences as well.

To be clear, there is nothing wrong with this. Fight scenes can be fun and tense without resorting to grievous bodily harm. However, if you want a grittier fight, give more visceral, specific bodily descriptions of the harm done and focus on evasion. The more generalised the verbs and adjectives are, the less gritty the fight scene will be to the reader.

You will also notice that authors choose to use a wider variety of verbs in fight scenes than they may usually. We do not use a different verb for speaking every time someone says something, but verbs can give the impression of a varied and interesting fight in a way that variations of 'said' do not accomplish for a scene with a lot of dialogue. Fight scenes are very physical, after all, and will involve extreme movements, whereas conversations do not always involve a wide variety of intonation and manners of speaking. Verb choice is often where we find character in fight scenes as well. A small person might 'scurry' while a large person might 'thunder'.

Playing to the strengths of the novel medium

A great book fight scene is not just a transliteration of a great fight scene from a film. They have different opportunities and tools available with the capacity to create vastly different sensory experiences. Relying too heavily on advice aimed at the film medium may mean you lose out on the strengths of the novel. We have already discussed using the reader's imagination, but another tool is using the subjective experience of the character. Books can get inside the head of characters far more than visual mediums can.

Frank Herbert's *Dune* is a peculiar study because of how much his fight scenes take place in inside his characters' heads:

> Paul pressed the fight now, circling but not attacking. He had seen the fear in his opponent. Memory of Duncan Idaho's voice flowed through Paul's awareness: 'When your opponent fears you, then's the moment when you give the fear its own rein, give it the time to work on him. Let it become terror. The terrified man fights himself. Eventually, he attacks in desperation. That is the most dangerous moment, but the terrified man can be trusted usually to make a fatal mistake.
>
> You are being trained here to detect these mistakes and use them.'
>
> The crowd in the cavern began to mutter.

They think Paul's toying with Jamis, Jessica thought. They think Paul's being needlessly cruel.

But she sensed also the undercurrent of crowd excitement, their enjoyment of the spectacle. And she could see the pressure building up in Jamis. The moment when it became too much for him to contain was as apparent to her as it was to Jamis . . . or to Paul.

Jamis leaped high, feinting and striking down with his right hand, but the hand was empty. The crysknife had been shifted to his left hand.

Jessica gasped.

But Paul had been warned by Chani: 'Jamis fights with either hand.' And the depth of his training had taken in that trick en passant. 'Keep the mind on the knife and not on the hand that holds it,' Gurney Halleck had told him time and again. 'The knife is more dangerous than the hand and the knife can be in either hand.'

And Paul had seen Jamis' mistake: bad footwork so that it took the man a heartbeat longer to recover from his leap, which had been intended to confuse Paul and hide the knife shift.

Except for the low yellow light of the glowglobes and the inky eyes of the staring troop, it was similar to a session on the practice floor. Shields didn't count where the body's own movement could be used against it. Paul shifted his own knife in a blurred motion, slipped sideways and thrust upward where Jamis' chest was descending--then away to watch the man crumble.

Jamis fell like a limp rag, face down, gasped once and turned his face toward Paul, then lay still on the rock floor. His dead eyes stared out like beads of dark glass.

Nearly half of this takes place inside Paul's head, weighing risks and contextualising every move to his character journey. This sort of introspection can give a lot of depth to a fight scene, a whole other dimension if you have the material for it. It is the difference between Brandon Sanderson writing the following in *Skyward*:

> My hand [hovered] as it reached for the eject lever between my legs… Screaming, I grabbed the lever and yanked hard.

And:

> I would not eject… I was NO COWARD! I was not afraid to die. And what will it do to them, something within me asked, if you do? … Screaming, I grabbed the eject lever and yanked hard.

The former feels more like watching part of a fight through a camera, while the latter is soaked in the subjective experience of Spensa, the protagonist. The former is still functional writing, it just lacks depth. Use the subjective experience of your characters to frame and give depth to the action.

<u>How do you balance internalisation and action?</u>

Stephen King pauses the fight we looked at before from *The Shining* for Wendy to internalise that her husband is truly going to kill her, that this moment is life or death for her:

> It came to her with sudden numbing reality that he meant to beat her to death with the mallet he held in his hands.

In *Dark Matter*, Blake Crouch only pauses the fight to internalise his protagonist's realisation that he is about to die:

I actually see my death coming, and I have no
words, just a fleeting image of me as a child on my
grandparents' farm in western Iowa.

Rowling pauses the fight as Harry internalises Sirius'
death:

He did not believe it, he would not believe it; still
he fought Lupin with every bit of strength he had:
Lupin did not understand, people hid behind that
curtain, he had heard them whispering the first time
he had entered the room—Sirius was hiding, simply
lurking out of sight—

What appears true for each of these is that internalisation
usually explores why the fight matters to the character; the
realisation or deep emotions that it is affecting them with. This
gives emotional weight to the action, making it more compelling.
Internalisation is rarely emotionally neutral; if it were it would
simply describe a character's thought processes.

The challenge here is to show rather than tell. This is such
an old axiom that it has almost lost its meaning, but it is true in
this case. It also leads us on to the second strength of the novel
medium: the five senses.

We usually focus on sight and sound because that is what
visual mediums use, but books use all five senses to help
immerse their readers. That fight in *The Hunger* brings up how
the man reeked of whiskey, and the sensation of swallowing grit.
These together give a different kind of realism, revulsion, and
anxiety to fight scenes that television and film struggle to attain.

Consider this passage in *The Girl with the Dragon Tattoo*:

He was about to pass out, and the pain in his
temples was almost unbearable. She turned to him
and saw that his face was the colour of a tomato, his

eyes were open wide, and his tongue was popping
out of his mouth… She stood on her toes and
frantically sawed at the leather strap to get [the
noose] off.

Larsson could have internalised this in saying, 'He knew
he was near death, and she knew she desperately had to free
him.' But instead, Larsson turns those thoughts into physical
movements, using sight and sensation to capture the feeling of
panic and desperation. The former shows us why the fight
matters through the memories and physical experiences while
the latter just tells us. Fundamentally, physicalise feelings with
the five senses where you can, and reserve descriptive
internalisation for those important story beats during the fight
scene. *Dune* pushes the boundaries of what most stories can
manage on this front without it becoming unpalatable, and it
seems most authors resist the temptation to go so far.

Dialogue

Almost every single one of the fights we have looked at
have some amount of dialogue involved. Much of it is utilitarian:
short, snappy, and to the point. When a fight is tense and evenly
matched, characters typically only say what is needed or what
comes out as a sign of anger, fear, or pain. In *The Poppy War*,
neither Rin nor Nezha say anything because they desperately
need to focus. Even in *Leviathan Wakes*, where there is a lot of
dialogue, the exchanges are all brief to reflect the tense, high-
paced speed of the situation, and every part of it is needed to
advance the action. They are a ship's crew, and much of the
tension comes from their ability to cooperate and communicate.
Even so, across the entire fight scene, there are only three lines
longer than two short sentences.

Dialogue in fight scenes is also often emotional, stripped
back to those base instincts that come out in moments of
adrenaline, raw and unfiltered. In *The Girl with the Dragon Tattoo*,
Salander only says one thing when fighting a serial rapist and

killer: 'Do you like pain, creep?' Her hatred for the guy comes through in a simple one-clause question as she beats him unconscious. It does not require a monologue about her traumatic past—this is not Shakespeare—and because it is so short, it does not break the pacing of the scene.

Despite this, plenty of stories do incorporate grand monologues into their fight scenes, and this is okay! Some writers like to conjure this more surreal, fantastical, even Shakespearean melodrama in their writing, and an extended speech can work well with that style. While we would not see it in *The Shining*, we might see it in your work. Plenty of characters will naturally speak during a fight because that is who they are. Prince Oberyn in *A Storm of Swords* is exactly this sort of character, and the books even make a point that his unnecessary flair while fighting is a flaw. It is ultimately his downfall, and the dialogue plays into this beautifully.

It is also worth noting that dialogue often crops up when there is either a shift in the balance of power or an extreme power imbalance. The character with the upper hand often speaks more. Just as detail can mark shifts in power in a scene, so too can dialogue; a particular character deciding to speak can represent them taking control of the scene. Dialogue and internalisation can both allow you to control the pacing of the fight scene. They can give the reader room to breathe. However, too much internalisation or dialogue can hamper the pacing as well. That balance is hard to strike, and I would refer you to the examples we have already discussed.

Scene structure

Moving on to discuss the macro of a fight scene, we should note that first and foremost, fight scenes are still scenes. They rise and fall in tension, have goals and resolutions, and a purpose and place in the narrative. The most common structure of a fight scene is to divide it into three acts: the fight begins, the fight is complicated or escalated, and the fight is resolved. Not exactly profound, but a useful framework for looking at fight scenes that might not be working. Consider the fight we discussed before from *Harry Potter and the Order of the Phoenix:*

1. Act I → the Death Eaters attack the young witches and wizards, demanding the prophecy.
2. Act II → the fight escalates when Hermione is hurt and Neville's wand breaks.
3. Act III → the fight reaches its highest stakes when Harry's friends are captured and he is surrounded. It is then resolved with the arrival of the Order.

Changing the stakes by complicating or escalating the problem the characters face multiple times like this makes for a more involving read. The obstacles change and actions have consequences. There is a rhythm to the fight that allows it to pack a bigger punch than if a threat was introduced, monotonous fighting ensued, and then everything turned out great. The eventual resolution—cathartic if it ends well, heart-breaking if it ends badly for our heroes—is made more satisfying by the struggle that comes from those complications and escalations.

This style of fight scene works well for a tense exchange between two sides, but this is not the case with every fight. A scene depicting a small, weak boy standing up to a bully may just involve him being repeatedly beaten down without the slightest suggestion he has a chance of winning. Escalation or complication are less useful here when the point of the fight is to demonstrate his character—that he is always willing to stand up to bullies, the consequences be damned.

However, I want to emphasise that you do not need pages and pages to escalate and complicate every fight scene. Alma Katsu does it in just two paragraphs in *The Hunger*: the fight begins when a man tackles Stanton to the ground, the fight escalates with the introduction of a knife, it is complicated by the dark and dust making things hard to see, it reaches highest stakes when he is about to be stabbed, and then is resolved when

Stanton gets the upper hand. The rise and fall within a couple of sentences makes this two-paragraph fight far more interesting than if it did not escalate.

In the section on where you should give detail, we discussed highlighting shifts in the balance of power or moments of narrative and character importance. The three-act structure fits in quite nicely with this because each of those points of escalation that complicate the stakes are usually accompanied by one of those three things. In *The Last Airbender*, Aang's final fight with Firelord Ozai is depicted partly in a series of disconnected compilations, but extra detail is given when the fight escalates at three points:

1. A significant character moment when Aang is forced to choose whether to kill Ozai with lightning. He decides to stick to his morals and refuses to. This also becomes a shift in the balance of power, which shifts against Aang, forcing him to flee and go on the defensive. The Firelord is pursuing him.
2. When Aang enters the Avatar state, gaining access to incredible powers that allow him to turn the fight on Ozai—the balance of power shifts. This is also a moment of narrative importance, as these powers have been inaccessible to Aang for a long time. It also raises the stakes and brings Aang into a new situation.
3. When Aang again refuses to kill Ozai, exits the Avatar state, and finds another way to defeat him. This is a significant character and narrative moment.

A second structure that I really like comes from KM Weiland's *Structuring Your Novel*, a book I can recommend as a great way to start understanding structure. In it, she gives a structure which gets you thinking about what is *around* the fight scene that makes it meaningful. We can call this the scaffolding of the scene.

The scaffolding of any given story beat can support it or undermine it, and this is true for fight scenes as well.

A lot of scenes can be broadly split into two categories: the active scene and the reactive scene. The active scene involves a goal, a conflict, and a disaster/resolution while the reactive scene involves a reaction, a dilemma, and a decision. Because writing is complicated, the line between these scenes will often get blurred. Not every active or reactive scene will follow each of these beats in this order, and sometimes it is helpful to consider them as six beats within a *single* scene. Personally, I find this more helpful. But the point remains that these beats are there to support the place and purpose of any given scene.

Let us consider an example. In GRR Martin's *A Storm of Swords*, the fight between the Mountain and the Viper to decide Tyrion Lannister's fate is what Weiland would call the active scene with a goal (win the trial), a conflict (the trial by combat), and a disaster (the Mountain kills the Viper at the last moment).

This active scene is followed by what Weiland would call the reactive scene. Tyrion sits in prison reflecting on how he is now condemned to death—reaction. He does not know what he can do to stop this—dilemma. He decides he will 'die with the taste of blood in my mouth'—decision.

While the active scene certainly holds weight on its own, this reactive scene gives extra depth to it by forcing character introspection. It allows the character to dwell on the consequences, internalise them, and then manifest them by taking a new path. The fight scene does not exist in the aether, having no bearing on what comes after it. It is not simply an obstacle that is overcome and used to add tension to a story thread, but a beat with emotional and narrative consequences that we explore. Structurally, pairing your active fight scene with a reactive scene gives the reader room to breathe as well, reflecting on the fight as much as the character does.

The point is this: if your fight does not demand a reactive scene, then what is its place in the story? Are you just adding fight scenes to artificially ramp up tension? A reactive scene does not need to be a character crisis. It might just be changing strategies, mild annoyance, or pride that they managed it so easily, but all these build scaffolding that support the fight scene.

Keeping it interesting

How do you keep a long fight scene interesting? Escalating and complicating a fight scene works well, but you can only do this so many times before you are building a third bigger, badder Death Star. What you will find is that battles like Pelennor Fields in JRR Tolkien's *The Return of the King* are structured around numerous small objectives: rally the troops, defend the gates, overrun the army, kill the Witch-King. Each of these allow for multiple escalations and de-escalations within the fight, fitting into a broader escalation and de-escalation pattern as they fail or achieve their objectives.

On top of this, longer fight scenes often use multiple characters who each have their own objective or struggle in the battle: Pippin, Merry, Eowyn, and Gandalf each have their own arcs in the Battle of Pelennor Fields. Gandalf succeeding in his by no means guarantees Eowyn will defeat the Witch-King, nor does it mean King Théoden will survive. These disparate objectives, successes, and failures emotionally complicate the fight.

In longer fight scenes, allow the reader the catharsis of objectives being achieved or failed, multiple releases of tension for better or worse. This will prevent inflicting tension fatigue on your reader, where every moment is treated as the most intense thing to have ever happened, even more intense than the last most intense thing to have ever happened. Without any release, tension can become tiring, even banal. De-escalation is important. The lull is scaffolding for more intense parts. It can even be weaponised against the reader by tricking them into thinking the tension is resolved and they can breathe a sigh of relief, only for the antagonist to return with a fury.

Fight scenes can also be made immensely more interesting if you think of them as problem-solving scenes. In *Leviathan Wakes*, James SA Corey establishes the problem right at the start of the fight: 'The Roci didn't have enough torpedoes for Alex to fire shot after shot at the station from far off and hope one made it through the point defense fire.' A puzzle: how do our heroes best use their very limited supply of torpedoes? The conflict in this scene is not just a shoot-out. Instead, it is a multi-dimensional problem for the characters to solve under pressure. The reader is engaging with the tension in multiple ways.

The *Pirates of the Caribbean* film series is famous for using this tactic. The iconic 'wheel' fight scene in its second film, *Dead Man's Chest*, involves a fight between three characters—Will, Jack, and Norris—who are not only fighting on a giant *moving* wheel, but each is trying to get away with the key to a chest *and* trying to figure who their real opponent is at the time. They are negotiating as they fight. Almost every fight scene in that series has a secondary problem-solving objective, and they are made even better when characters are forced to choose between multiple objectives. Do I kill the person or get the macguffin? Do I save the girl or fulfil my debt?

Does the fight scene really matter?

Author of *The Greenbone Saga* Fonda Lee puts it like this:

'For a fight to have meaning, it must be essential to your story. Throwing in fights just to keep the reader's attention and the action quotient high is something that Hollywood is often guilty of, but you don't want to emulate a forgettable popcorn flick. Ask yourself what the purpose of the fight scene is. Is it to reveal character? To set up a crucial plot point that will have ramifications later? … If you remove the fight scene, does the storyline completely fall apart? It should.'[2]

We discussed before how a good way to judge this is whether the fight demands a reactive scene. Sometimes we add in conflict just to spice the story up with a bit of action and a side of death, but that is not always optimal. Another, and perhaps a more potent way to judge, is by identifying the question your fight scene is really asking beyond whether the characters will get out alive.

As Jack Torrance is hunting Wendy Torrance down, the fight is not simply asking whether Wendy will get out alive, but whether there is any humanity left in Jack. The final fight in Brandon Sanderson's *Skyward* asks whether the protagonist Spensa will let go of her ego and eject from her flightcraft after refusing to do so previously. *Harry Potter and the Order of the Phoenix* is asking whether Harry will learn the prophecy made about him. A good fight is not merely an obstacle to the next story beat but helps develop a deeper narrative or character question as it ensues. The most common way this is done is by forcing the character into a crisis moment in their arc.

I do not take as hard a line to fight scenes as Fonda Lee does. I do not feel your story *needs* to fall apart if you take away a fight scene, but I do think it is worth critiquing your work from this perspective and identifying the logic underpinning your narrative beats.

Magic systems

Authors writing stories with hard magic systems are often so focused on showing how cool their system is that they leave theme and character behind in the climax. Instead, it becomes a showcase for the brilliant and unique ideas they have. Climactic

---

[2] Fonda Lee "Blow-by-blow: 5 tips on Writing Action and Fight Scenes" (7 October 2015) Writer's Digest <www.writersdigest.com>

fight scenes tend to be far more satisfying if they have character and thematic depth first and magic system cool-ness second.

A lot of this is to do with *when* these elements come to fruition. Identify the moment of greatest tension in your climax and ask what the text explores: is it a major character moment, a reveal about your magic system, or even both? Letting both elements be resolved at the same time can work well, but the reader will know if the highest point of tension does not align with the cumulative point in your character's arc. It can subtextually indicate the magic system is either more important or more consequential than the payoff to your character arc.

It can be hard to communicate how your magic system works—often leading to laborious, taxing, and boring segments of exposition that the reader does not care about. In *On Writing and Worldbuilding Volume I,* we discussed how to deliver exposition more effectively, focusing on obscuring it within scenes of conflict, tension, or surprise. Fight scenes fit into this mould quite well.

My one caution to offer here is that a fight scene is not interesting simply because it is a fight, and a conflict with no consequence does not feel like much of a conflict. That does not necessarily make it bad, but it can be obvious what the author is doing. To return to our discussion on active and reactive scenes, a fight scene that demands a reactive scene is a brilliant avenue to slip in some of this magic system exposition.

Fights earlier on in your story can also play the role of Chekhov's gun—introducing a vital piece of information that will come back later. One of the most well-known examples would be the magic of sacrificial love in *Harry Potter and the Deathly Hallows.* Having established during the fight with Voldemort in *Harry Potter and the Philosopher's Stone* that Harry's mother dying to save him gave him a magical protection against Voldemort, it is revealed that Harry giving up his life for his friends protects them from the spells of the Death Eaters and Voldemort as well. By introducing these elements of your magic system early on, you can use them later for a brilliant payoff.

These moments can also be used as a kind of foreshadowing known as a pre-scene. This shows the reader a smaller version of an event that will happen again on a much larger scale later. The example you will likely be most familiar with is Luke Skywalker closing his eyes and trusting the force to help him deflect a couple of lasers about half-way through *Star Wars: A New Hope*, then later trusting the force to help him destroy the entire Death Star. The former is a pre-scene of the latter, setting up a rule in the magic system which supports the payoff in the climax because George Lucas did not need to explain it.

Realism

A fight scene not being realistic is a common critique but writing a realistic fight scene does not necessarily make it a good fight scene. In GRR Martin's *A Storm of Swords*, Bronn takes on Ser Vardis Egan, and it is a lot more realistic than most fight scenes with swords and armour. Martin highlights how heavy armour is, that it weighs Ser Vardis Egan down and makes him slower, and that Bronn's height gives him extra reach—which is a fundamental advantage in close combat—and how the narrow slit of Vardis' visor limits his vision. These elements are set up and paid off when they end in Ser Vardis' death.

The main benefit of realism is it helps with credibility and believability in fiction, allowing you to then build on that with more creative and fantastical elements which we buy into. However, it would be overly restrictive to say a good fight scene *must* be realistic. A lot of authors like to write surreal, fantastical, melodramatic, and awe-inspiring combat that captures us with its unreality. The wuxia 'martial heroes' genre has a long history of surrealist fighting, as do comics and anime.

There is value in the unreal as much as there is value in the real.

Summary

1. Whether using short or long sentences, shorter action beats maintain fast pacing and tension in a fight.
2. Verb chains work best when supported by a sense of cause and effect and chronology. This can be achieved with the react-pause-act and goal-conflict-disaster structures, which also bring variation to the fight scene.
3. Not every moment of a fight should be detailed. Detail works well where the power balance shifts, where characters get closer or further from their goal, or in important narrative or character moments.
4. Generalised descriptions and creative language allow the reader to get the feel and flow of the fight in non-essential moments.
5. Establish the physical environment before the fight, especially set pieces that later become complications in the fight. This helps the reader follow the action and assists in building up tension prior. You only need to track the physical movements of characters with important story beats in the fight.
6. Using specific bodily descriptors in describing pain and blows makes the fight feel grittier and more brutal. This is usually accompanied by an emphasis on evasion. More generalised descriptions can bring a lighter tone.
7. Subjective experience can give depth to the action. Internalisation usually arises from exploring why a fight matters to a character, and it is usually written with emotive language. Otherwise, physicalise these thoughts with the five senses.
8. Dialogue during fight scenes is often snappy and to the point, emotional, or reflective of a power imbalance. However, the biggest factor is character. These are guidelines, not rules.

9. Fight scenes are still scenes. Consider using the three-act structure with multiple escalations. Escalations work well when paired with a power shift, narrative importance, or character importance.

10. Ask whether your fight demands a reactive scene that gets the character reflecting on it, even if only in a small way.

11. Longer fights use numerous objectives that allow for de-escalation—success or failure for the characters. They also often give multiple characters different objectives. De-escalation is important.

12. Looking at a fight as a problem-solving scene will make it immediately more multidimensional and interesting, especially if characters must choose between multiple goals. Figure out what question the fight scene is really exploring.

13. Do not let your magic system eclipse character or story in a climactic fight. Fight scenes are excellent for introducing pieces of exposition or foreshadowing.

HANDLING PACING

The Bourne Identity by Robert Ludlum
The Rest of Us Just Live Here by Patrick Ness
Elements of Fiction Writing by James Bell
Worth Dying For by Lee Child
The Perks of Being a Wallflower by Stephen Chbosky
Beyond: Two Souls developed by Quantic Dream
My Heart and Other Black Holes by Jasmine Warga
Romeo and Juliet by William Shakespeare
It's Kind of a Funny Story by Ned Vizinni
Sufficiently Advanced Magic by Andrew Rowe
Numinous by Michael Wright
Beartown by Fredrik Backman

Pacing is the speed of experience of events for the reader in your story. Fast pacing is not necessarily good pacing; going slow is important too. Good pacing is about knowing which parts of your story need to feel fast and which parts need to feel slow.

There are two levels to pacing in a story that we will deal with today:

1. Micro pacing → The minutiae of pacing a particular scene.
2. Macro pacing → The pacing of the overall narrative.

A lot of pacing advice focuses on that first level of minutiae, and while it is important to discuss, we will narrow in more on that less understood second level of pacing.

Micro pacing

Sentence structure and grammar can be used on a paragraph-to-paragraph basis to accelerate or slow the pacing. Consider this section from Robert Ludlum's *The Bourne Identity*:

> He was crouched by the wall. Jason stood up and fired; at the sound of his gun, the beam swung over to him. He was the target; two shots came from the darkness, a bullet ricocheting off a metal strip in the window. Steel punctured his neck; blood erupted.
> Racing footsteps. The executioner was running toward the source of the light.

Short, punchy sentences move through events quickly, giving the feeling of speed. Sentences are action-reaction—'Jason stood up and fired; at the sound of his gun, the beam swung over to him'—the instant switch between decision and consequence to compress time. Ludlum uses short clauses; there is no time to ponder for character or reader. The language is sharp and clear rather than poetic. Drawing on those techniques we discussed in Chapter One on fight scenes, Ludlum uses visceral bodily descriptors—'Steel punctured his neck'—to create a very real fear of bodily harm. This chapter also finishes on a cliffhanger. All these techniques together give the reader the feeling they are moving through events quickly, making them want to turn the page because any sentence could be the character's last. These techniques are most easily exemplified in action scenes, but they can be applied to any scene of high tension.

In contrast, consider this scene from Patrick Ness' *The Rest of Us Just Live Here*:

> Back when I first went to the hospital on the night of the accident, Steve gave me this oil to put on my

scar to keep it from stretching and getting bigger. I
often get caught in a loop with it, rubbing it in,
wiping it off, rubbing it in, wiping it off, until I'm
sure I'm doing far more stretching damage to the
scar than would have ever happened by just using
my face.

These sentences are longer, more complex, lingering on
actions and full of introspection like we are travelling at the
same speed the character is thinking. There is repetition and
poeticism, taking page time to articulate the feeling beyond the
action with greater space between action and reaction, between
cause and consequence.

Whichever you use, both fast and slow-paced techniques
are broadly aimed at mimicking the experiences of the characters
in the patterns of your writing. Fast-paced writing patterns give
the reader the feeling that there is no time to stop and think,
while slowly paced writing patterns give emotional beats more
weight by allowing the reader to simmer in them for a while. It
facilitates introspection in your character by letting the reader
feel the emotional turmoil for longer and emphasising the
difficulty of character growth—that it takes time and thought.
Forcing the reader through such things too quickly would make
the decision or trauma feel inconsequential or easily resolved.

While it is true that pacing is intricately tied to tension, this
understanding of pacing techniques does lead to a
misconception that moments of high tension always require fast-
paced writing, which is simply not true. James Bell discusses
what he calls 'Stretching the Tension' in *Elements of Fiction
Writing*:

'Lee Child squeezes an amazing amount of
tension out of a few seconds because he's not at all

afraid to make us wait. And that's the key to
tension. It is waiting. The longer the better.'[3]

Consider this passage in Lee Child's *Worth Dying For*:

> Reacher saw the dark blue Chevrolet and
> instantly linked it through Vincent's testimony back
> at the motel to the two men he had seen from
> Dorothy Coe's barn, while simultaneously
> critiquing the connection, in that Chevrolets were
> very common cars and dark blue was a very
> common color, while simultaneously recalling the
> two matched Iranians and two matched Arabs he
> had seen, and asking himself whether the
> rendezvous of two separate pairs of strange men in
> winter in a Nebraska hotel could be just a
> coincidence, and if indeed it wasn't, whether might
> then reasonably the presence of a third pair of men,
> which might or might not be the two tough guys
> from Dorothy's farm, however inexplicable those
> six men's association might be, however mysterious
> their purpose, while simultaneously watching the
> man in front of him dropping his car key, and
> moving his arm.

This passage describes Jack Reacher calculating and
moving to throw a single punch. Child uses sharp, non-poetic
language, but he also allows for detailing Reacher's thought
process, adding longer clauses and sentences that dwell on his
thought patterns. He slowly introduces more complicating
details and factors that increase the tension but put a massive
distance between the action and reaction, all to make that
action—throwing the punch—more consequential when it
finally happens. He 'stretches the tension' because it suddenly

---

[3] James Scott Bell *Elements of Fiction Writing — Conflict and Suspense*
(Writer's Digest Books, United States, 2012).

feels like there is a lot more riding on this one punch than there ever would be if Child just wrote, 'Reacher recognised the two men following him, and immediately spun, throwing a fist into the first man's chest'. Fundamentally, these are more guidelines than rules for where you should use these techniques.

Bell's sentiment to stretch the tension is true to an extent. It is why waiting to reveal who the serial killer is in a thriller is so satisfying; the wait gives it payoff. But using this stretching technique too often can weaken its effect, resulting in a slow, ploddingly paced scene when it should feel tense. If you want to use this technique, then consider using it at only a few especially important moments of high tension.

James Bell's advice is also wholly sound for stretching emotional tension. In Stephen Chbosky's *The Perks of Being a Wallflower*, we spend a lot of page time inside Charlie's head, delving into the mind of a mentally unwell teen struggling with his friendship group breaking apart. The author does not just say Charlie had a breakdown and move on. He stretches the emotional tension for over a dozen pages, putting a huge gap between action and reaction. Prolonged emotional turmoil is something we can all relate to, that feeling of being stuck and not knowing what to do, of dwelling endlessly on our emotions. We can feel paralysed. This slow-burn emotional intensity is important for making whatever path the character does take feel truly impactful in stories that primarily derive tension from internal crisis. It is only after Chbosky shows us Charlie repeatedly saying he is totally fine that we read his thoughts spiralling and suddenly ending up at:

> I'm so sorry that I wasted your time because you really do mean a lot to me and I hope you have a very nice life because I really think you deserve it. I really do. I hope you do, too. Okay, then. Goodbye.

Chapter close.

Emotional beats like this can rarely be action-reaction. Stephen Chbosky does remove grammatical breaks we would normally expect like commas and semi-colons to create the sense of unstoppable thoughts, but this is supported by pages of slower and still very tense introspection beforehand.

When you find emotional moments happening during fast-paced scenes, you will often find the author switches their writing style to dwell on them.

These micro techniques deal with the visceral feeling of a scene, but you can have fast and slow scenes that work well on their own and still not have a well-paced story. You have probably heard the advice to 'keep the story moving', and one way your narrative can come to a grinding halt is with what we will call the Sidequest Problem.

The Sidequest Problem

If you have ever played a video game, you will be familiar with the kind of quests where your hero has a goal to do [z]. Maybe he needs to slay the dragon that killed his family. But to do that, he needs the Sword of Reckoning—we will call this goal [y]—but to get that he needs to find the Temple of the Sky—we will call this goal [x]—but to do that, he needs to convince a witch to tell him where it is—we will call this goal [w]. The structure of the game's narrative becomes this:

Starting point → goal [w] → goal [x] → goal [y] → end goal [z].

This kind of storytelling manufactures obstacles between the player and the end goal that feel arbitrary and are aimed at lengthening the game without too much complexity. Even though you are doing things as the player, you do not feel like you are moving the story forward because these obstacles are largely meaningless. The only one with a personal dimension is goal [z]: slaying the dragon. We will assume these obstacles do not reveal anything or pose moral dilemmas for our characters.

The result is bad pacing. It feels unnecessarily slow and drags regardless of how tough it is to get the Sword of Reckoning or kill the Guardian to the Temple of the Sky because the reader does not feel like the core narrative is moving forward. The core narrative as a character's personal journey to do [z] is just stalled.

If this was a book, there would be words on the page, but they would not be saying anything. Director and writer Ryan Koo highlighted one reason for Pixar's storytelling successes: 'Simplify. Focus. Combine characters. Hop over detours.' On an experiential level, these manufactured obstacles and sidequests are detours from the main narrative. You could take out obstacles [w] to [y] and you would not lose anything of value because there is no real narrative reason for these obstacles to exist. What would it matter if our hero already had the Sword of Reckoning? This is the Sidequest Problem, and it happens in books as well.

When considering the pace of your overall narrative, figure out which obstacles make your ending more meaningful and which ones could be removed. Does the obstacle:

a. fundamentally alter the ending

b. fundamentally develop your main character's arc

c. reveal something new about the world or story

If not, then does it need to be there? If it is a grey area, consider combining that obstacle with another story beat that does serve one of these purposes. James Bell discusses the pacing of a subplot by comparison in saying:

> 'A subplot, by interacting with the main story line, adds complications (at least, it should)... by way of emotion [or] physical means [with] the subplot charging right into the main plot wreaking all sorts of havoc.'[4]

---

[4] James Scott Bell *Elements of Fiction Writing — Conflict and Suspense* (Writer's Digest Books, United States, 2012).

In Shakespeare's *Romeo and Juliet,* the main plot is the romance between eighteen-year-old Romeo and thirteen-year-old Juliet. The rivalry between the Capulets and Montagues is a subplot because it invades the main plot by complicating their relationship. It plays an intricate role in their character arcs and fundamentally alters the ending by culminating in their deaths. If it were a sidequest, then Romeo and Juliet would just need to defuse tensions halfway through the story to meet up one time, only for the rivalry to never resurface, never alter their character arcs, and not change the ending.

In our example, acquiring the Sword of Reckoning does not require our hero to change, it does not change the ending from what we would expect, and it does not reveal anything new about the world. It does not charge right into the main plot wreaking all sorts of havoc. Not all obstacles are subplots, but they justify themselves in similar ways.

Analysing your obstacles in this way can help the narrative continually move forward by only including obstacles that complicate and deepen the story. Whether written to be fast-paced or slow, sidequests do not really give any pace to the core narrative because it is functionally brought to a standstill. It is for this reason that flashbacks often feel out of place. Too often authors bring them in at a time that does not serve one of those three purposes.

The 2013 game *Beyond: Two Souls* developed by Quantic Dream is a narrative-driven game about a girl with psychic powers finding herself and avoiding those who would abuse her abilities. Chapter Fourteen is called 'Navajo', and it details her ventures when she joins a small Native American family living in the isolated Midwest. It is an incredibly long and slowly paced chapter to the point of being one of the most unenjoyable parts of the game by its end. The main character, Jodie, does evolve as a person by the end of it, but she does not change nearly enough to justify the huge time investment the player is asked to give to this obstacle. We do not uncover any new information in the mystery nor do its events alter the ending in a truly meaningful way. There is not enough payoff in terms of moving the core narrative forward. It is badly paced. As mentioned before, in grey areas like this, it may have been well worth combining the Navajo obstacle with another to give it more narrative development.

<u>The Big Thing</u>

What I am getting at here is that good pacing for your core narrative is about whether the reader feels they are getting closer to the 'Big Thing'. In a mystery like Thomas Harris' *Red Dragon* this is whether we are getting closer to catching the serial killer. In Jasmine Warga's young adult novel *My Heart and Other Black Holes*, this is whether Aysel is getting closer to resolving her suicidality. When editors tell us that we need a fast-paced beginning, they are not talking about opening with a fight scene or argument, or even using those fast-paced techniques we discussed before. They are talking about how quickly the author puts the reader on the track towards the Big Thing.

This is done with the hook, a question, the first twist or reveal in the inciting incident. Then after that, how quickly does the reader feel they take to reach the next step towards the Big Thing the author introduced? Slower pacing of a narrative, usually throughout the second act, slows down page time between these 'steps' towards the Big Thing. What is the Big Thing in your story, and when does the reader get their first, second, and third real tastes of it?

<u>Subtext</u>

Editor September C. Fawkes brought up something I had not considered before: how a lack of subtext can undermine pacing.

'I was once editing a manuscript that had all the
right beats and emotional draws… But it felt slow

and boring… I discovered it was because it had next to no subtext, and… I wasn't intellectually invested in understanding and figuring out the text.'[5]

Subtext enriches a story because whether consciously or subconsciously, the reader is continually investigating the text for extra meaning. It is an understanding the text hints at or gives implicitly. It is reading between the lines. Without subtext, the pace can slow down because there is less information being delivered in the same words and there is less intrigue for the reader to ponder and uncover. Consider the following passage from Ned Vizinni's *It's Kind of a Funny Story*:

> 'You all right, man?'
> This should be my name. I could be like a superhero: You All Right Man.
> 'Ah…' I stumble.
> 'Don't bug Craig,' Ronny is like. 'He's in the Craig-zone. He's Craig-ing out.'
> 'Yeah.' I move the muscles that make me smile.
> You see how words work? They betray your mouth and walk away.
> 'Are you okay?' Nia asks…
> 'I'm fine,' I tell her.

The abstraction of Craig's feelings from his smile tells us about his true emotions and something about his depression. On the surface, the events of the story tell us Craig is fine, but the way it is written tells us there is something seriously wrong and he is not okay. If used intelligently, subtext can help the reader feel like every scene is getting them closer to the Big Thing, even when what is happening on the surface may not feel like it is directly contributing to the ending.

---

[5] September C Fawkes "8 Common Pacing Problems" (September C Fawkes: Write better with an editor) <www.septembercfawkes.com>

Fantasy and science fiction stories have a particular hurdle to overcome here: pacing with worldbuilding. Whether it is details about the magic system, the politics, religion, or otherwise, unless woven expertly into your story, worldbuilding can seriously hamper the pacing of the narrative by forcing the reader to stop and learn about the roses. Andrew Rowe's *Sufficiently Advanced Magic* features a complex magic system, and though enjoyable, it can be criticised for the stop-start pacing of its fight scenes. They lose a lot of tension because Rowe segues away from an emotional or action beat to remind the reader how the magic system works in the middle of characters doing things.

This is not a chapter on succinctly delivering exposition. There is a chapter on this in *On Writing and Worldbuilding Volume I*. However, what is worth noting is that when worldbuilding halts the pacing of a scene, it tends to be because the author feels they need to explain something so the scene makes sense. Sometimes this is necessary, but most of the time it is not. If you need to do this repeatedly, then chances are either you are not trusting your readers to be smart enough to know what is happening or you have not explained things sufficiently beforehand.

Worldbuilding that works with the pacing supports the emotional beats of the scene. Consider this piece from Michael Wright's *Numinous*:

> As much as the intricate lines and patterns were beautiful, they all meant nothing. The sanctum tower in Bailing Bell was made in the image of one of Gena's great towers before they had fallen. But it was all form without function here; only designed to try and echo how the first towers looked, and this tower even did a poor job at that. As much as Nym wanted to laugh at the people's attempt at reproducing one of Gena's great works, it only made the immortal sad.

The emotional beat here is an immortal reflecting and longing for a golden age when a godlike being ruled the continent, now only a shadow of its former glory. This beat helps us understand who the character is, and the worldbuilding describing the architecture supports that emotional beat. Go through your worldbuilding segues and ask if they interrupt or support the emotional beat, and whether you are trusting your readers enough.

Finally, we will talk about pacing and genre. What defines good pacing is not universal.

Structure and pacing conventionally work together with a fast first act, slower second act, and fast third act. While broadly true, different genres thrive on different speeds of pacing because people get invested in stories in different ways. The contemporary young adult genre is an interesting case study. Slow-paced writing is important for investing readers in the personal arcs of your characters. It takes time to examine their thoughts and feel the consequences of their decisions and mistakes in a way that fast-paced writing is not as equipped to do. Contemporary fiction authors, especially in young adult fiction, lean hard on this tactic because this is how their readers often get invested in a story—often through issues they can personally relate to like depression and suicide. Deep psychological introspection is what they are there for. It is also why it is a lot more common to find first-person narration in contemporary young adult fiction. Like slower-paced writing, it complements that method of getting readers invested.

Compare this to the writing of Lee Child or Robert Ludlum—authors in the spy and thriller genres which lean hard on fast pacing. They attract different audiences, and while fast-paced scenes do happen in young adult stories, the actual events of the story tend to be less immersive for that readership than the deeply personal psychological journey. There is not the same need to be pulled along and thrilled at every turn, but instead a desire to be understood, represented, and empathised with. This can result in a slowly paced first, second, and even third act.

The Rest of Us Just Live Here by Patrick Ness is a young adult story told from the perspective of those who would normally be background characters to the real story. Ness writes almost intentionally against the expected framework of a story, including in his pacing. It is a slowly paced book across all three acts. Where you expect the story to pick up in some great conflict at the end, it simply fizzles out—after all, they are not the main characters. Their stories are deeply ordinary, and life does not follow a three-act structure.

For most of the book, Mikey's narration is full of long, lumbering sentences that can feel meandering; conversation feels aimless on the surface, but all of this is intentional. These techniques give a heaviness to every thought and action of Mikey, a depressing weight where life feels futile and out of his control, playing into this fear that everybody is growing up and moving on except him. To a lot of readers of the young adult genre, this kind of subtext and introspection is very immersive. They simply would not get as much from fast-paced writing as readers of Ludlum and Child would.

Fredrik Backman's *Beartown* is a contemporary adult story about the people in a small town in the middle of nowhere. Everybody knows everyone, and everyone's decisions affect everyone else. It has one of the largest casts of characters it expects you to remember in a single book I have ever read. To call it a 'slow burn' would hardly capture it. The first two-hundred pages are spent introducing you to each of these characters, their lives, and the way of life in Beartown. Even when the events of the story pick up, the book remains slowly paced for the most part. Backman was writing for a particular type of reader interested in a deeply realistic depiction of life, including its lulls, and as a result, conventional pacing would not have worked as well.

Fundamentally, good pacing is also about the audience you are writing for and the kind of tension you want to cultivate. Telling you to write a fast-paced first act, slower second, and fastest third would not be good advice because different stories will work for different folks. Because of this, I think the more helpful lens of analysis is whether readers feel they are getting closer to the Big Thing. In fast-paced spy thrillers, this can be saving the world, while in slow-paced contemporary fiction this can be a deeply personal depiction of loss or dissociative identity disorder.

Summary

1. You can alter the micro pacing using sentence structure, word choice, action-reaction framing, and other techniques like cliffhangers, introspection, and removing filter words.[6]

2. High tension does not necessarily mean using fast-paced techniques. However, stretching the tension too often can dull its effect.

3. The Sidequest Problem arises when plot obstacles have no narrative reason to exist, slowing the pacing of the core narrative, or at worst, halting it entirely. Consider whether an obstacle fundamentally alters the ending, complicates the core narrative, develops your main character, or reveals something about the world or story.

4. A subplot complicates the main plot, supporting fast pacing by adding tension or slowing pacing by adding emotional character moments, while a sidequest breaks the pacing of the core narrative.

5. Subtext enriches the reader's experience by accelerating the pace because the reader is continually following implicit points of intrigue and investigating the text for deeper meaning.

6. Worldbuilding segues work when they support the pacing by underpinning emotional beats. Segues that interrupt the pacing often occur because authors do not

---

[6] Filter words are discussed in detail in the chapter on first person writing.

trust their audience enough or have not made the required exposition clear enough.

7. Good pacing is dependent on genre, with action novels or thrillers leaning fast and contemporary young adult leaning slow. Know your audience.

WRITING MENTOR
CHARACTERS

Creating Character Arcs by KM Weiland
The Testaments by Margaret Atwood
Ready Player One by Ernest Cline
The Giver by Lois Lowry
The History Boys created by Alan Bennett and Nicholas
Hynter
Revenge of the Sith directed by George Lucas
Harry Potter and the Prisoner of Azkaban by JK Rowling
A Clash of Kings by GRR Martin
A Game of Thrones by GRR Martin
The Librarian of Auschwitz by Antonio Iturbe
Artemis Fowl and the Opal Deception by Eoin Colfer
American Gods by Neil Gaiman
The Dragon Prince created by Aaron Ehasz and Justin
Richmond
How the Grinch Stole Christmas by Dr. Seuss

The mentor character is an old and easily recognisable archetype. The image of the old grey-haired man leaning on a staff with a twinkle in his eye leaps to mind as it leaps from the page. Typically, we explore the mentor character through their relationship with the protagonist, and because of that, this chapter will examine their conventional role in the narrative as the character arc catalyst.

We will split this discussion into nine parts: the type of insight, mentors and negative arcs, the action-reaction scene, the emotional opposition scene, the lesson-action scene, humanising mentor characters, design, and killing mentor characters.

Type of Insight

By nature, the mentor character espouses some form of insight that the protagonist does not yet have, but what kind of insight do they need to possess? In KM Weiland's fantastic book *Creating Character Arcs,* she brings up the Lie the Character Believes:

> 'He is harbouring some deeply held misconception about either himself, the world, or, probably, both... Your character may not even realize he has a problem.'[7]

Consider what relationship your mentor character has to your protagonist's Lie. The role of that relationship will change depending on whether the character has a positive arc—changing for the better—or a negative one—changing for the worse, as well as whether the mentor is a positive or negative influence.

In a positive arc, the mentor has a specific insight into the Truth that the protagonist does not yet believe. In Margaret Atwood's *The Testaments,* Aunt Lydia acts as mentor to Aunt Victoria—a devout supplicant in the Republic of Gilead, a dystopia soaked in religious fundamentalism that was born from the ashes of the United States. Aunt Victoria believes wholeheartedly in the righteousness of Gilead, that women should be under the leadership of men, and that women are to blame for inflaming the desires of men if they show their bodies.

---

[7] KM Weiland *Creating Character Arcs: The Masterful Author's Guide to Uniting Story Structure, Plot, and Character Development* (PenForASword Publishing, United States, 2016) at 26.

This is the Lie she believes and Aunt Lydia mentors her towards the Truth.

Aunt Lydia does not just espouse the odd piece of wisdom relevant to the plot like a hint from a Dungeon Master, nor does she know the answer to every problem in the story. Aunt Lydia herself knows a specific and important Truth about life critical to Aunt Victoria's character arc: Gilead is corrupt, that women deserve equal respect and liberties, and that they are not to blame for the actions of men. In the end, Aunt Victoria finds this liberating. Her view of herself and of the world is radically changed for the better. The specificity of the mentor's insight is important because it is what makes the mentor-protagonist dynamic effective. Rather than nebulous ideas about equality, equity, and faith, Aunt Lydia gives specific lessons that let the protagonist view their experiences in new ways. The applicability of these lessons also makes change in the protagonist more believable.

Insight can seem hollow if it does not characterise major emotional differences between the protagonist and their mentor. Ernest Cline's *Ready Player One* uses James Halliday as a mentor figure for Wade, even depicting him as a grey-bearded wizard, yet the advice he espouses is vague, and there is no real sense that Halliday has learned a lesson Wade needs to learn himself. There was no strong sense that Wade, the protagonist, believed a Lie where the mentor believed the Truth. Nor was there any sense that Halliday was more emotionally mature than Wade, yet the story still treated him as somehow wiser and more learned. Cline expected us to give Wade some credence he did not deserve.

In contrast, in Lois Lowry's *The Giver,* readers can clearly see emotional differences between the Receiver of Memory, who has learned the truth of the horrors of war, torture, and humanity's history, and the protagonist Jonas, who learns them across the story. Where Jonas lacks emotion, the Receiver is full of passion and pain. It is a story that asks whether it is better to know, feel, and remember the painful things in life or not feel at all. With this, we should note that knowing the Truth does not need to necessarily make one happier. Jonas becomes emotionally distraught when he learns it, feeling all the pain and ecstasy that humanity has forgotten. Aunt Lydia is full of confidence and conviction, believing in her own self-worth, whereas Aunt Victoria starts out unconfident and berates herself for her lack of conformity.

It is quite common in darker adult fiction and dystopian stories for the Truth to mean the central character learning they live in a darker reality than they ever believed. In *The Giver*, Jonas learns that his home in the Community is built on a terrible lie and coming to terms with this generates a lot of internal conflict. In *The Testaments*, Aunt Victoria talks about the destruction of her faith in a heart-wrenching passage:

> I feared I might lose my faith. If you've never had
> a faith, you will not understand what that means.
> You feel as if your best friend is dying, that
> everything that defined you is being burned away;
> that you'll be left all alone.

Despite this, the protagonist does not technically need to accept the Truth that the mentor believes for them to undergo a positive arc. In the 2006 film *The History Boys,* a class is mentored by Hector, who believes that education is valuable for education's sake. That whether poetry is valuable in an office space in New York does not matter because the poem is worthy of remembering on its own. This is his Truth. While the boys do come to see that there is value in Hector's worldview, and the boys grow as people because of it, a different mentor also encourages them to view education as something that sets them up for life financially, a tool giving them more freedom in the long run. Both Truths are good things to learn but neither represent the totality of their characters' arcs. Each boy comes to his own conclusion.

This is because a mentor character does not need to have the *whole* Truth and nothing but the Truth. They could be wrong, not know a lot of things, or be right about only one crucial thing that matters to the protagonist. This depiction of the mentor is less common, with authors preferring the paragon archetype, but it is one with a lot of potential. A lot of modern deconstructionist stories like *The Last of Us Part II* and *The Last Jedi* have opted for these flawed mentor characters. Nobody in our lives, from parents to teachers to role models, has the whole Truth to life. The Truth is always insight from a combination of people. Seeing where the mentor gets it wrong can make them more human, relatable, and real.

Aunt Lydia, the Receiver, and Hector are examples of mentors in a positive change arc, but what about negative change arcs?

Mentors and negative arcs

A mentor in a negative change arc may either guide the protagonist towards the Truth which they ultimately reject, leading to their downfall, or they may mentor the character towards a Truth which manifests in negative change. We see the former in Obi-Wan Kenobi as Anakin's mentor in *The Revenge of the Sith*. Anakin rejects the Truth of the Jedi way to attain power that the Jedi refuse to use and teach. The Emperor is the rare case where a mentor guides the protagonist towards a Lie. The dynamics we have discussed so far in this chapter are simply inverted in this case.

That first dynamic is usually the most tragic, especially when the mentor's actions cause the protagonist to reject the Truth. Their acceptance of the Lie can be rooted in the flaws of the mentor, often either because the mentor does not empathise with their struggles enough and alienates them or the mentor forces them to make a decision that they have not yet matured enough to make.

In most mentor relationships, the mentor pushes back against the worst inclinations of a character and fosters their positive inclinations in the hope of bringing them to the Truth, but this runs into a problem John Truby recognises in *The Anatomy of Story*:

> 'You never want to create characters that sound like a mouthpiece for your ideas. Good writers express their moral vision slow and subtly, primarily through story structure and the way the hero deals with a particular situation.'[8]

We already discussed how the mentor's specific Truth should characterise emotional differences between them and the protagonist, but how does the mentor bring the protagonist to understand the Truth without becoming a walking, talking thematic mouthpiece? How do they *mentor* the protagonist? We will discuss three important types of scene you can use: action-reaction, emotional opposition, and action-lesson.

The action-reaction scene

The action-reaction scenes were previously discussed in Chapter One on fight scenes. To repeat our definition: the active scene involves a goal, a conflict, and a disaster/resolution while the reactive scene involves a reaction, a dilemma, and a decision. Because writing is complicated, the line between these scenes will often get blurred. Not every active or reactive scene will follow each of these beats in this order, and sometimes it is helpful to consider them as six beats within a *single* scene. Personally, I find this more helpful.

Mentors naturally slot into this scene structure: they help the protagonist get past at least one of the six steps that they would be unable to alone.

To demonstrate, consider the structure of this exchange in JK Rowling's *Harry Potter and the Prisoner of Azkaban* where

---

[8] John Truby *The Anatomy of Story: 22 Steps to Becoming a Master Storyteller* (FABER & FABER, United States, 2008).

Harry, the protagonist, wants to learn how to conjure a patronus with the help of his mentor, Professor Lupin.

> GOAL: Harry wants to learn to conjure a patronus.
>
> OBSTACLE: Harry must face a boggart in the form of a dementor.
>
> RESOLUTION: Harry fails, and the boggart renders him unconscious.
>
> REACTION: Harry blames himself and thinks of himself as weak.
>
> DILEMMA: Harry must decide whether he can continue.
>
> DECISION: Harry decides to continue.

It is in working through these steps that the protagonist sees a little more past their Lie. Professor Lupin helps Harry work through the reaction and dilemma steps. He talks with Harry about hearing his parents' voices, helping him process those flashbacks, and weaves in the Truth he is trying to teach him: that being traumatised does not make him weak and that he can always hold on to his happiest memories in the darkest of times. It is only by learning this that Harry manages to beat back the boggart.

Do not take this as a hard and fast rule. This scene is an unusually exact example of the action-reaction scene. Plenty of stories mix up the order and weight of each of these beats, or even miss some entirely. Forcing your mentor scenes to conform to this structure can even make them more awkward instead of letting them flow in the way you feel the interaction would naturally go. While it may be more common for the mentor to step in during the reaction and dilemma steps, it is also possible they would fit in at any of the other steps. Imagine if Lupin helped Harry find a new goal more in line with the Truth, or by saving him during the resolution/disaster, Harry learned something by watching Lupin.

The emotional opposition scene

This technique is a lot more subtle and simple than the other two. It is where the protagonist ends up in a different emotional state to where they were at the beginning of the scene, and the mentor helps them reach that point. For example, consider this scene where Jonas experiences the memory of family love in *The Giver*:

> Jonas did not want to go back. He didn't want the memories, didn't want the honour, didn't want the wisdom, didn't want the pain. He wanted his childhood again, his scraped knees and ball games... But the choice was not his. He returned each day to the Annex room.
> ... Jonas opened his eyes and lay contentedly on the bed, still luxuriating in the warm and comforting memory. It had all been there, all the things he had learned to treasure.
> 'What did you perceive?' The Giver asked.
> 'Warmth,' Jonas replied, 'and happiness. And — let me think. Family... I liked the feeling of love.' [9]

At the beginning of the scene, Jonas does not want anything to do with becoming the next Receiver. He is distraught, hopeless, and has broken down. He finds the pain of the memories simply too much to handle. Come the end of the scene, Jonas is hopeful once again. The Giver has brought him to see the value of love and family—something the Community has lost.

The emotional opposition scene is a simple but effective way of showing how the mentor contributes to the emotional arc of the main character. They question where those emotions come

---

[9] This scene also involves a lengthy discussion about family structures, omitted for brevity.

from, both positive and negative, and offer new ways of looking at things that inspire different emotions. In a sense, they have a wider view of the world and events, and emotional opposition scenes show us how the protagonist's emotions come from a narrower view of the world and of themselves they are yet to dispel. When considering the emotional differences between the protagonist and mentor, this is where they would come out most heavily. Jonas would not have felt this way had he the full experiences and wisdom of the Giver.

The mentor here takes action that subverts the expectations of the protagonist, confronts them, and causes emotional change. It gives the mentor more agency than the action-reaction structure necessarily does. The subversion comes from them acting on the Truth they know that the protagonist does not. In the case of *The Giver*, the Giver is totally capable of going on with life, laughing, and being happy where Jonas finds he is not. But this is only because Jonas does not yet know the feeling of love — something even more beautiful than warfare is terrible. By showing Jonas these beautiful things — the Truth — he can bear the weight of the terrible memories and continue on.

In this way, the emotional opposition scene can leave the protagonist feeling positive, but these scenes can also leave the protagonist feeling worse. In *A Clash of Kings* by GRR Martin, Cersei Lannister mentors Sansa Stark in the Red Keep during a bloody battle that they are losing. Sansa begins fearful but hopeful. Cersei then shocks her by talking about how she hates her role as queen mother and what she knows is about to follow:

> '… But if Maegor's Holdfast should fall before Stannis can come up, why then, most of my guests are in for a bit of rape, I'd say. And you should never rule out mutilation, torture, and murder at times like these.'
> Sansa was horrified. 'These are women, unarmed, and gently born.'

> 'Their birth protects them,' Cersei admitted, 'though not as much as you'd think. Each one's worth a good ransom, but after the madness of battle, soldiers often seem to want flesh more than coin.'

Cersei knows the Truth about knights and war. She breaks down the naïve Lie of the noble fight that Sansa believes in. By the end, Sansa is left demoralised.

> 'The only way to keep your people loyal is to make certain they fear you more than they do the enemy.'
> 'I will remember, Your Grace,' said Sansa, though she had always heard that love was a surer route to the people's loyalty.

Sansa's actions are based in the naïve Lie; Cersei's actions subvert her expectations because they are based in the Truth that she has yet to learn. Sansa's arc is that of becoming a skilled and politicking courtier, and sometimes, learning the Truth on the way to that can hurt.

The action-lesson scene

You have seen these a million times before. The action-lesson scene is where the protagonist attempts something, it goes horribly wrong, and they must then learn where they went wrong. The mentor character is the only one who can teach them this. It is the most direct a mentor can usually be when it comes to espousing the book's themes and the Truth—especially when it is merely the mentor sharing wisdom rather than them acting. Relying on these scenes too much can come across as heavy-handed.

These scenes typically work best when failure is an emotional experience for the protagonist, and that failure allows them to believe, accept, or understand a Truth that they could not before, rather than it being a case of them just not having heard. Having the protagonist go, 'Well, if I knew I should believed in myself, Mr Greybeard, then things would have turned out different!' is not that fun. Failure works well when it reflects the protagonist's flaws, not their ignorance.

There is nothing inherently *wrong* with an action-lesson scene where the mentor simply tells the protagonist a thing they need to learn, even without the failure step. The reason to avoid it is that it is simply not as effective as the action-reaction or emotional opposition scenes. In an action-lesson scene there is little emotional weight attached to the advice, and it is worth asking whether you want that, and whether you are delivering the information in the optimal way.

One interesting subversion of this scene is where the mentor gives the lesson before the protagonist is emotionally ready, leading the protagonist to reject it or even inspiring them to do the reckless thing they advised against. In GRR Martin's *A Game of Thrones,* Jon Snow's mentor Maester Aemon tells him that, 'The men [of] the Night's Watch... must have no divided loyalties to weaken their resolve.' This advice causes Jon to abandon his duties when he learns his father figure Ned has been executed. He wrongly decides to be more loyal to his House than to the Watch because he was not ready to internalise Maester Aemon's advice. This would have ended in his execution for desertion had he not been taken back by his friends. Only after making the mistake of leaving does he see the value in firming up his loyalties to the Watch, setting the stage for his story from that point on.

Humanising mentor characters

Are your mentor characters people? If you are not careful, mentors can turn into banks of infinite wisdom: you slot in a coin of personal failure and they just happen to pump out the right fortune cookie. They can lack flaws, wants, or needs that traditionally make characters human, or those things can be superficial, playing little if any a role in the narrative. The result can be an inhuman mentor character.

You can use the action-reaction scene to explore the mentor's flaws, needs, and wants. In the scene from *Harry Potter and the Prisoner of Azkaban* we discussed before, Harry experiences flashbacks to his parents when he takes on the boggart-dementor. As Lupin helps Harry process this and recover during the reaction beat, Harry asks about Lupin's relationship with both Sirius Black and his father:

> 'Professor Lupin?' he said. 'If you knew my dad, you must've known Sirius Black as well.'
>
> Lupin turned very quickly.
>
> 'What gives you that idea?' he said sharply.
>
> 'Nothing — I mean, I just knew they were friends at Hogwarts too…'
>
> Lupin's face relaxed.
>
> 'Yes, I knew him,' he said shortly. 'Or I thought I did. You'd better be off, Harry, it's getting late.'

Lupin is momentarily taken aback and set on edge before acquiescing. While he admits to knowing Sirius, he clearly avoids any further questions by insisting Harry should head off. This beat humanises Lupin by showing him to keep secrets, that he is not always calm and contemplative, as well as giving him meaningful relationships, feelings of betrayal and pain and self-doubt. We see that he *wants* his friends back, who are either dead or accused of murder at the time.

By tying the mentor's flaws to any of the six beats in the action-reaction scene (though most commonly the reaction beat), you can simultaneously develop the mentor alongside the protagonist. Perhaps they talk about their own struggles during the reaction or how they faced a similar decision during the dilemma.

A similar thing can be achieved with the action-lesson scene. Phrasing the action-lesson scene as an exploration of the mentor's mistakes—showing the protagonist their scars, literal and figurative—helps the scene feel less like a moralistic sermon and more like a genuine emotional connection between the characters, despite delivering the exact same information. It allows you to avoid the fortune cookie machine trope and shows that the mentor went through growth too.

Secondly, we discussed before how the mentor might only have part of the Truth. Occasions where they are wrong can act as a great flaw for their character, especially if it plays a consequential role in the story, causing harm to the protagonist, themselves, or others. Consider how the Truth that the mentor does not know might complicate your story, either leading the protagonist astray or causing conflict between the two characters. This is precisely what happens in *The History Boys,* and it truly serves to humanise Hector as a mentor.

Thirdly, you can give your mentor character their own arc. A cynical mentor returning to the fight, understanding sacrifices must be made for the greater good, that girls are just as worthy of training as boys. The list goes on and on. An extreme example can be found in Antonio Iturbe's *The Librarian of Auschwitz* where Hirsch, a leader amongst the Jews, responsible for starting schools inside the camp, has an arc ending in his suicide. Dita Adler spends much of the novel trying to uncover *why* Hirsch ended his life. Though he taught Dita the Truth about how to retain dignity in the face of such indignity, his own personal struggles bested him in the end with major consequences for the story. The school is left without a true leader. The mentor's arc shapes the challenges, personal struggles, and conflicts the protagonist faces.

This works especially well when the protagonist challenges them in their own way. In this sense, it becomes a two-way relationship of teaching and learning, through which they both grow together. Which elements of your protagonist might confront the mentor with a Truth they need to understand, and which events in the story might confront the mentor emotionally on that arc?

Killing the mentor

It feels like the mentor is all too often killed because the author wants the protagonist to grow up. Because they need to be making the plot decisions for once. Think *Eragon's* Brom, *Star Wars'* Yoda, and Duke Leto in *Dune*. This is not necessarily a bad trope, but it is only one of many purposes the mentor's death can serve in the narrative.

There are plenty of other ways to force the protagonist into independence. Separation from the mentor forces the protagonist to decide for themselves whether they put their mentor's advice into action. Lack of accountability always changes things. Perhaps it is only in embracing the wisdom of the mentor that the two characters are truly reunited. This also means that the protagonist doing the right thing carries more weight because they willingly chose to follow the mentor's advice because it is worth following.

Some authors use the mentor's death as a plot catalyst, a tool for establishing theme, or to establish the villain. Hirsch's death in *The Librarian of Auschwitz* acts as the inciting incident for much of Dita Adler's story. Eoin Colfer uses Julius Root's death in *Artemis Fowl and the Opal Deception* to motivate Holly Short and establish how big of a threat Opal poses compared to any of the antagonists they have faced before. Opal took down Julius Root when even Artemis could not—the genius and mastermind who had so far bested the fairies in every way. Wednesday's death in *American Gods* is vital to understanding the themes of life and death Neil Gaiman wants to explore—that power comes from sacrifice, and that death of the mind is more important than death of the body.

It can be interesting to have the mentor's death result from their flaws, needs, and wants, complicating the sacrificial trope we are so used to. In Aaron Ehasz's *The Dragon Prince*, King Harrow is killed because of his warmongering past and how he underestimated his enemy. Interestingly, this death does not motivate our heroes to act; they do not even know it has happened. Instead, it is used for dramatic irony, with one character keeping the secret of his death from them. This becomes a source of tension later in the story.

It needs to be said though: the fact that Gandalf was killed by the Balrog in 1956 does not make the death of *your* mentor less meaningful. Killing the mentor will still be a strong emotional beat if we care about the relationships the mentor character had. If the reader sees this relationship as a vital part of the protagonist's emotional makeup, then they will care. How many times has a romantic lead been dramatically killed off, despite *Romeo and Juliet*?

Designing the mentor

I have always been a big proponent of the idea that originality comes less from the aesthetic of a character and more from their function within the narrative. Just because the mentor is an old, sagely, white dude does not make him a cliché if he plays a sufficiently unique role. Even so, falling into those tropes as a default can make your characters unnecessarily similar to others. Do consider alternative sources of wisdom for the character. In Dr. Seuss' *How the Grinch Stole Christmas,* the old, cynical protagonist is mentored by the young and optimistic Cindy Lou. Wisdom and strength come with experience, and experience is limited to no demographic.

Summary

1. The mentor has specific insight into the Truth that the protagonist cannot see. It can be effective to show the emotional differences between them because of this — positive and negative. However, the mentor need not have the whole truth. They may be wrong about some things, and the protagonist may find their own Truth, building on that specific insight.

2. In a negative change arc, the fall of the protagonist is sometimes facilitated by the flaws and mistakes of the mentor, often by not empathising enough or by forcing them to make a decision they are not ready for, causing them to reject the Truth.

3. In the action-reaction scene, the mentor teaches the protagonist by helping them get past one of the six steps that they could not by themselves. This is often the reaction or dilemma step. This technique avoids moralising to the reader.

4. In the emotional opposition scene, the mentor acts based on the Truth that subverts the expectations of the protagonist because they still believe the Lie. This causes emotional change across the scene. This can make them feel better or feel worse as the Truth can be hard to learn.

5. In the action-lesson scene, the mentor helps the protagonist by directly espousing a moral platitude, sometimes following a failure of the protagonist. This is most effective when it is a Truth they could not have accepted without the emotional experience of their failure first. One subversion of this is the mentor telling the protagonist something before they are ready to hear it, causing them to do the reckless thing, leading to failure.

6. Mentors are commonly humanised in three ways: using the action-reaction or action-lesson scene to explore their flaws, past mistakes, wants, and needs, exploring the consequences to the partial Truth they have, and giving them an arc of their own.

7. Killing the mentor is an understandable move to force the protagonist to mature, but it can help to give it a second purpose in the narrative. It will still be an emotional beat in the story if the author shows how they are vital part of the protagonist's emotional makeup. Likewise, consider unexpected sources of wisdom in designing your mentor character.

POSITIVE ARCS AND REDEMPTION ARCS

King Lear by William Shakespeare
A Christmas Carol by Charles Dickens
Avatar: The Last Airbender created by Mike DiMartino and Bryan Konietzko
Captain Spirit developed by DONTNOD
Beauty and the Beast directed by Gary Trousdale and Kirk Wise
Ender's Game by Orson Scott Card
A Song of Ice and Fire by GRR Martin
Les Misérables by Victor Hugo
The Return of the King by JRR Tolkien
The Kite Runner by Khaled Hosseini
Speaker for the Dead by Orson Scott Card
Return of the Jedi directed by George Lucas
Harry Potter and the Deathly Hallows by JK Rowling

When we think of redemption arcs, we think of characters going from villain to hero, but it is not that simple. People are complicated, and anyone, even heroes, can do terrible or misguided things that they feel they need to be redeemed from. A character does not need to be a what-if-we-just-let-the-kids-die villain to need or want redemption. In Shakespeare's *King Lear*, Lear is a complex character—a good king but a selfish father, generous but self-obsessed, brave but prone to fits of anger. Across the story, he undergoes a redemption arc for his actions that fracture the kingdom and lead to the horrific death of his daughter Cordelia. Across his arc, he gains humility, patience, and empathy.

Despite our inclination to put redemption arcs in a category of their own, the truth is they are merely a subset of the positive arc where a character changes for the better. The emphasis is on terrible acts they have committed or being on the 'bad' side, yes, but the change is still rooted in their values, priorities, and beliefs changing for the better as they come to see through the Lie the Character Believes, finding the Truth. Almost everything discussed in this chapter can be applied to positive arcs more generally because the story dynamics are the same in many cases. Where redemption arcs differ is mostly in the emphasis on redemption and what that means.

How redemption arcs begin

Your character may begin their story at any point along their path to redemption. Perhaps they have just decided to make a change, or have made changes already, or they are on the verge of total redemption, or perhaps they do not even see the need for redemption yet. Wherever your character starts, it is worth considering how they got to the point they are at:

1. The character begins without feeling any remorse or guilt and does not comprehend their wrongs at all. Think Scrooge in Charles Dickens' *A Christmas Carol*. Scrooge not only never gives a thought to how his selfishness affects others but laughs when these flaws are pointed out to him.

2. The character partly comprehends their wrongs, but they continue to do wrong out of misplaced priorities. Prince Zuko from *Avatar: The Last Airbender* is one such example: he wants to act honourably but wrongly believes that honour comes from his abusive father's approval. In efforts to impress him, he hurts others.

3. The character acknowledges their wrongdoing but struggles to stop doing the bad things. Think Charles Eriksen in DONTNOD's *Captain Spirit*. Charles hits his son when he drinks, hates himself for it and wants to stop, but in a cycle of addiction, he cannot drop his alcoholism, leading to more abuse.

Any of these setups are used for both protagonists and antagonists, but the second and third ones tend to make for more relatable and likable protagonists because they at least acknowledge their wrongs. Remorseless psychopathy is, unsurprisingly, harder to empathise with for most people. Scrooge is the protagonist, but we all hate him at the start.

A helpful tool to use here is what we are going to call the Positive Arc Trifecta:

1. what your character feels is at stake for them
2. how they view themselves
3. how they view the world

These things are intimately connected with why your character acts the way they do, and throughout their story the way the character was acting beforehand will become incompatible with how they come to see the stakes, themselves, and the world. In *Beauty and the Beast*, the Beast is full of selfishness, self-pity, and you might say mild anger issues. He treats Belle and her father terribly and needs to be redeemed from this life of cruelty and selfishness.

> STAKES: The Beast wants to be left alone to wallow in self-pity.
> SELF: The Beast views himself as irredeemable and unlovable.

> WORLD: The Beast sees the world as cruel and
> having abandoned him.

As his story progresses, each of these things change. Come the end, the Beast does not want to be alone and *wants* Belle to love him, he believes himself capable of good things, and the Beast sees that the whole world has not abandoned him, even if there are some terrible people out there. Acting with anger, selfishness, and self-pity is no longer compatible with his views of himself, the world, and the stakes. Because of this, he feels he must change the way he acts towards others, and this culminates in his eventual redemption.

How does your character's view of the stakes, themselves, and the world around them change across the story?

<u>Making a convincing change</u>

No reader or author wants this change to come out of nowhere, so let us consider three possible story threads you could use to develop this change trifecta.

1. Confronting the character with the reality and gravity of their actions →

In Orson Scott Card's *Ender's Game*, Ender starts out believing that the use of excessive force to prevent future conflict is justified. This culminates in him becoming unwittingly responsible for the total genocide of an alien species known as the Buggers when he is given command of humanity's space fleets. It is only afterwards that Ender learns that the Buggers were not mindless animals but sapient creatures like humanity. This confrontation with the consequences of his beliefs and actions put him on the path to redemption as he tries to find a new home for the last Bugger queen in *Speaker for the Dead*. This sharp confrontation can be a powerful emotive scene where the character realises what they were truly doing to others, how they downplayed the consequences and harm of their actions, or that they were wrong all along.

2. A radical shift in circumstances that changes their perspective →

This is exactly what happens to Jaime Lannister in GRR Martin's *A Song of Ice and Fire*. Jaime goes from being the greatest swordsman in the finest armour feasting in castles to a handless prisoner spending time amongst the smallfolk. Through this ordeal, Jaime is humbled and begins seeking ways to deal with conflict other than violence. This can force a character into a position that their victims would have been in previously. This inversion naturally leads them to understand, empathise, and want to change their ways. Alternatively, the radical shift could simply remove the advantages they are accustomed to, à la *Schitt's Creek*, forcing them to reconsider how they solve problems and their values. Finding new solutions can lead to character change.

3. A character enters their life and pushes them to change →

This trope often manifests in either a woman, as in *Beauty and the Beast*, or a child as in James Mangold's *Logan*. In both cases, a character traditionally associated with optimism, innocence, and purity smooths out the crinkles of anger, spite, and isolation in a man. These characters are typically a foil, bearing traits that contrast with the character in need of redemption, and act as a counterweight to their worst impulses. In developing this relationship, the character begins to view themselves, the world, or the stakes more like this new character does, culminating in redemption as they change their ways.

Zuko's redemption arc

As a longform example, let us examine how all these things function in Prince Zuko's redemption arc in *Avatar: The Last*

Airbender. At the beginning of his story, Zuko is at war with himself. He partly comprehends his wrongs but continues to hurt others and himself out of a misplaced sense of the stakes and an incorrect view of himself and world.

> STAKES: Zuko wants his father's love, approval, and his honour.
> SELF: Zuko views himself as dishonourable and weak because honour and strength come from displays of raw power.
> WORLD: Zuko views the Fire Nation as spreading prosperity through the war.

To him, these things justify him burning down villages and rejecting love and friendship. As with the Beast, across the story, his trifecta gradually changes.

> STAKES: Zuko wants to choose his own destiny, and to be loved by those who appreciate him.
> SELF: Zuko sees himself as honourable and finds strength in humility, kindness, and love.
> WORLD: Zuko understands the Fire Nation is a tyrannical, warmongering, genocidal power waging an unjust war.

The first thing to begin changing is how he views himself. With the help of his mentor Iroh, he begins to question what makes him honourable. Despite believing that power, obedience, respect, and conviction are the most important expressions of honour, as early as episode twelve of the first season, Zuko recognises that he should put the safety of his crew before his need to appease his father. He even apologises for doing so.

The seed is planted; the kernel grows.

This naturally feeds into his view of the world changing. Seeing kindness and compassion as important to being honourable means also recognising the harm caused by the Fire

Nation. They are being neither kind nor compassionate in their war.

The stakes are the last thing to change. Though his idea of honour becomes more complicated, almost right through to the end, Zuko cannot separate his idea of honour from his desire for his father's approval and regaining his position as Crown Prince. Eventually, these stakes become incompatible with his evolving views of himself and the world: his father's approval will mean hurting others who do not deserve it and regaining his title will mean supporting a war he now knows to be unjust. One of these must give way. With this, Zuko realises that what he *truly* needs is to carve out his own destiny and that he does not need his father's approval. It is ultimately a story of want versus need.

To reach this point, the writers repeatedly place Zuko in positions where his old conceptions are challenged. In the famous episode *Zuko Alone*, he finds himself in a poor rural Earth Kingdom town kept under the thumb of some thuggish earthbenders because the 'real soldiers are off fighting in the war'. Villagers do not speak about the war with hope or a sense of adventure and glory but fear that their loved ones will die. The episode ends with the farmer that Zuko befriends learning his son has been killed. The war is stripped of the propagandistic, glorious pretences he was raised with. He is also forced to choose between laying low or defending the town but finds he cannot turn a blind eye anymore. His honour demands he defend the helpless.

Zuko's arc is also facilitated by two of those story threads we discussed before: a major shift in circumstances—he is stripped of all titles and hunted down by his own family—and being confronted by the reality of his actions. It isn't simply personal reflection that leads to change but exposure to new stimuli and challenges he has never had to deal with before.

Failure makes success meaningful

Breaking deeply harmful habits and wants is hard, and
failure to do so is fundamental in a redemption arc. Not only
does it add tension to the story, letting the reader question
whether the character can overcome their worst impulses, but it
makes their eventual triumph over their darker nature
meaningful. This will manifest in small things at the beginning
of their arc—small acts of kindness that cost them little—and
then greater things later in the story that cost them a lot.

Structurally, failure also plays an important role in the rise
and fall of tension across the whole story. A gripping and
convincing redemption arc will not look like a linear graph
trending upwards from badness to goodness. There will be
bumps, falls, spikes, and pits as the character fails to resist their
worst urges. When creating the specific decisions that the
character will fail or succeed in making, it may be effective to
place big decisions with consequences at the end of each act with
smaller decisions spaced in between. The darkest hour plot beat
often aligns with a great failure after much progress, only for
them to achieve redemption in time.

In *Beauty and the Beast,* the Beast repeatedly falls back into
habits of irrational fury, self-pity, and isolation. He gets
unreasonably angry at the smallest of things. Yet even after
making a measure of progress in trying to be patient, waiting for
Belle at dinner and ensuring she has everything she could need,
he flies into a fit of rage when he finds her in the West Wing,
throwing her out of the castle. Then, though he remedies this by
saving her life, he keeps her in the castle against her will.

This back and forth gives weight to his eventual decision to
let her go free, sacrificing his one chance at returning to human
form at the same time. It is also worth noting that *Beauty and the
Beast* shows how redemption does not necessarily mean
happiness. It can mean living with the consequences of your
wrongs. It can mean becoming disillusioned with a world you
used to be happy in. The Beast sinks back into despondency and
self-pity during the darkest hour of the story when Belle leaves,
but this is also the moment of his redemption—not, contrary to

popular understanding, the transformation at the end of the
story. It is because only in letting Belle go does the Beast truly
understand what he wants: not to be human again, but to be a
good person and to be loved freely.

Failure can also be an effective motivator; the character
gives in to their view of themselves or the world and finally
gains what they thought was at stake, only for it turn to ashes in
their mouths. The reader and character can finally see how
hollow what they wanted truly is, leading them to question what
they actually need. It also shows them what they have lost after
improving for so long. Victor Hugo's *Les Misérables* features half
a redemption arc in Javert, who gets what he wants: Jean
Valjean, notorious criminal, at the mercy of the law. Yet, in his
moment of triumph, he finds himself unable to carry out the
sentence.

> One thing had amazed him, — this was that Jean
> Valjean should have done him a favor, and one
> thing petrified him, — that he, Javert, should have
> done Jean Valjean a favor.
> Where did he stand? He sought to comprehend
> his position, and could no longer find his bearings.
> What was he to do now? To deliver up Jean
> Valjean was bad; to leave Jean Valjean at liberty was
> bad. In the first case, the man of authority fell lower
> than the man of the galleys, in the second, a convict
> rose above the law, and set his foot upon it. In both
> cases, dishonor for him, Javert.

Instead, he is left questioning his views of himself and his
views of the world—what it means to be just and how just the
law is as an institution. Unable to let go of what he wants—
justice under the law—and unable to quite see what he needs is a
new understanding justice, Javert ends his own life. In many

stories, this would lead to a radical change in worldview and his eventual redemption, but Hugo resisted this.

What would happen if your character got what they think they want? This can work great as a darkest hour plot beat, or as a way to complicate the second act.

Failed redemption arcs are less common for a reason. There is a catharsis to seeing a character fulfil their potential and seeing a character you love reach the place they need to be. Failed redemption arcs can risk undermining what your reader loves in a character; it can feel hollow if it feels like there is no purpose to their suffering and eventual failure. Even so, you should write your arcs how you want them and not to fit some advice from someone who does not understand your vision.

With this said, some notable failed redemption arcs have worked because they serve a wider thematic purpose. Gollum's near redemption and failure in *The Return of the King* plays a significant role in Tolkien's theme of evil being destined to destroy itself. The intense desire the Ring creates in those who possess it may be part of the reason its evil survived so long, but it is also the reason it is destroyed: Gollum cannot resist it and he dances over the edge, full of ecstasy created by the Ring. Gollum's failed redemption helps us understand that just like evil, the Ring destroys itself. For Victor Hugo, the inflexibility of the law, and thus Javert, was thematically important to his work.

The meaning of redemption

Developing a convincing character change is only one half of writing an arc like this. What does it mean for a character to be 'redeemed'? Is it enough for them to simply stop doing bad things? This is a subjective question, but I find the most convincing redemption arcs employ a degree of literary symmetry. This is where the character takes redemptive action throughout the story that reflects their wrongs or failings in the past. It results in a sense of poetic justice.

One way to do this is by showing the character make a decision that they could not have brought themselves to do before — often by echoing a choice in the first act with a choice in the third act of the story. In Khaled Hosseini's *The Kite Runner*, the character Amir feels intense guilt after choosing not to intervene to protect his friend Hassan in the first act. Hassan also loses his life protecting something of Amir's. The third act of the novel deals with Amir's redemption as he chooses to intervene to save Hassan's son from an abusive orphanage.

Here, redemption is gained through action that directly reflects where the character failed before in the story. It resonates emotionally because it shows the character has come to deeply understand the harm they caused before. Merely recognising the harm is not enough for me. Mending relationships and preventing further harm are also part of it. This also fits nicely with the 'radical shift in circumstances' story thread. There, a character is placed in symmetrically opposed circumstances — often the position of those they had previously wronged — giving them the perfect reason for acting differently in the future: they know what it is like to be on the receiving end of their injustices.

There are different types of redemption. Hamlet's redemption is wholly personal while much of Jean Valjean's arc is about him gaining redemption in the eyes of society and God. Many such arcs are about gaining redemption in the eyes of those a character has harmed. The dramatic tension in the former comes heavily from the 'views of himself' arm in the trifecta. *Hamlet* is full of introspective scenes where Hamlet is torn three different ways about himself. Is he mad? Is he a failure? Is he jealous? He believes his indecisiveness is a moral flaw that allowed Claudius to take over. Come the final act, it is satisfying to see Hamlet feel he has redeemed himself, even if it culminates in his death. Ender knows he cannot gain redemption in the eyes of the world in *Speaker of the Dead,* so he tries for some measure of redemption in the eyes of the last Bugger queen by finding her a new home world.

This discussion would not be complete without mentioning the extremely common, sometimes lazy, but always fun trope 'Redemption Equals Death'. This is where a character has a change of heart and sacrifices themselves for the greater good, supposedly redeeming themselves in the process. Think Darth Vader.

Simply having the character die often lacks that element of symmetry. Darth Vader's sudden turn in *Return of the Jedi* to sacrifice his life to save Luke does not mean he has grasped the horror and trauma he has inflicted on millions, and it does not mean he truly regrets what he did. As far as the audience is concerned, Vader arguably only cares when his actions hurt someone he cares about. That is not much of a redemption.

It also assumes giving up one's life is the most meaningful thing one can do to face up to their past. While noble, they also escape the consequences of their actions by not having to face the victims, mend relationships, or deal with ongoing guilt, all of which are arguably more meaningful and more relatable for an audience who has never experienced death.

This does not mean death cannot be a compelling element of the character's redemption, but that is what it is for me: an element. One small cog in a working machine of redemption. In *Harry Potter and the Deathly Hallows*, JK Rowling reveals Severus Snape has spent years atoning for his sins by protecting Harry. This includes saving him several times and letting the world view him as a traitor by killing Dumbledore to help Harry fulfil his destiny in defeating Voldemort. In the end, these efforts lead to his death. For Snape, redemption was purely in the eyes of Harry and his mother, Lily. While Snape does treat Harry awfully for years in many ways, his death is still an effective part of this redemption. Death is a full stop at the end of a long, complex, compelling sentence in a nuanced redemption arc.

It is worth noting that just because a character has reformed themselves does not mean everyone around them believes it or trusts them. Mending relationships and righting wrongs is complicated, and most characters would not have seen them undergo their psychological change. Perhaps a character is unwilling to forgive them after what they did. Sometimes, trauma stays with us to the point that forgiveness is impossible. You cannot always undo the harm you have done, and there is a space in stories for characters to never forgive. If someone is traumatised and they forgive flippantly, it can feel dismissive of their pain and suffering from a meta-textual perspective, where readers were expecting it to more deeply factor into how they relate to the 'redeemed' character.

Summary

1.   Redemption arcs are a type of positive arc. They typically begin with the character either not regretting their actions at all, comprehending some wrongs but continuing to do wrong out of misplaced priorities, or they understand their wrongs but struggle to stop, sometimes because of addiction.

2.   Consider how a character's view of the stakes, themselves, and the world change across the story. It is these competing new and old perceptions that drive the inner conflict resulting in positive change. Change is often made more convincing when they are confronted with the consequences of their wrongs, when radical changes in their circumstances shift their perspectives, or when a character with opposing views of them, the world, and the stakes challenges them.

3.   Allowing the character to make mistakes is more relatable, convincing, and emotionally engaging. It adds tension through the possibility of failure. It can be effective to structure this around two similar choices— one in the first act and one in the third act—with the character making a different, better decision at the end. Giving the character what they think they want can be a

fascinating plot beat as they grapple with how hollow
the reality is.

4. Failed redemption arcs are less common because they
can feel unsatisfying after building up the character
growth for so long. However, they can work if they
serve another narrative purpose like articulating theme.

5. Effective redemption arcs often entail poetic justice and
symmetry. Symmetry helps show the character's deep
self-reflection and understanding of the harm they
previously caused. The death equals redemption trope
often lacks symmetry. However, that does not mean it
cannot be done well when used as a final beat in a more
comprehensive arc.

POWER ESCALATION IN A MAGIC SYSTEM

The Stormlight Archives by Brandon Sanderson
The Matrix directed by Lana Wachowski and Lilly Wachowski
Seven Deadly Since by Nabaka Suzuki
The Magicians series by Lev Grossman
Artemis Fowl and the Last Guardian by Eoin Colfer
Artemis Fowl and the Opal Deception by Eoin Colfer
Mistborn: The Final Empire by Brandon Sanderson
The Riftwar Saga by Raymond E Feist
A Wizard of Earthsea by Ursula Le Guin
Jessica Jones created by Melissa Rosenberg
The Kingkiller Chronicles by Patrick Rothfuss
The Dark Knight directed by Christopher Nolan

Perhaps your main character is a wizard. We will call him Graham. Across the story, his powers are going to grow. He starts out pulling bunnies from hats—not a hugely useful combat ability—and by the end he is shooting lightning from his fingertips. As his abilities escalate, it is the writer's job to make this escalation believable, compelling, and to avoid the many pitfalls along the way.

This chapter will be split into six sections: character arc-aligned power escalation, escalation and tension, power creep, power ceilings, incomparables, and character challenges.

<u>Character arc-aligned power escalation</u>

The first common way to handle power escalation is to
integrate it with character arcs. This trope goes way back to
mythological tales of only the righteous, strong king being able
to draw the sword from the stone, and then even further back
than that. In Brandon Sanderson's *The Stormlight Archives*,
Dalinar and Kaladin each slowly attain new abilities like those of
a mystical order called the Knights Radiant, but they can only do
so in accepting and living up to certain ideals. Kaladin gains new
abilities when he accepts that protecting others means he should
protect even those he hates.

This technique means that power escalation aligns with the
growth of your characters, and this can be a great way not only
to ensure that character development is always front and centre,
but that abilities feel earned. Overcoming obstacles means
overcoming personal issues, biases, and character flaws. The
flow of the tension in the story is more cohesive because the
internal and external conflicts are fundamentally connected. It
can give external conflicts emotional weight as well as manifest
internal conflicts in a visceral way.

Part of this technique is structural: stories that use
character arc-aligned power escalation will usually mean that
failure to defeat the antagonist or master an ability happens at
the same time as moral or personal failure. The 1999 film *The
Matrix* features Neo, who must learn to stop letting the digital
world of the Matrix control his perception, and instead must use
his mind to manipulate the Matrix. When he fights Morpheus, he
believes he loses because Morpheus is too fast. Morpheus
challenges that idea:

> 'Do you think that my being stronger or faster has
> anything to do with my muscles in this place?'

It is only when he begins to control his own perception of
the world around him that he can manipulate the Matrix and
beat Morpheus.

But it is not as simple as giving a power up to your characters whenever they become a better person, like the universe hands out good Samaritan coupons. It is important to let characters fail when they try to use these powers, because just like failure is what makes moral struggles more compelling, failure to use parts of the power system are what make their eventual mastery so satisfying. This is especially true if failure has major consequences for their emotional journey. To continue with *The Matrix* as an example, at the climax of the film, Neo is shot. This seemingly kills him because he is unable to fully put mind over body. It is only with Trinity's love that he manages to overcome it and survive, returning to the Matrix with full mastery over his own body and mind, fulfilling his potential.

Character arc-aligned power escalation is sometimes inverted where escalation becomes a failure of character. *Seven Deadly Sins* by Nabaka Suzuki features a character called Meliodas who has virtually unlimited power at his fingertips if he gives into anger and rage. The challenge for characters like this—often overpowered in that emotional state—is to *not* give in to those emotions, or to find alternative ways of solving problems.

It may be easy to defeat the antagonist, but incredibly difficult to remain a good person in doing so. It connects to the thematic idea that power costs your humanity. Power escalation in these stories is given narrative weight by seeing how the escalation affects the protagonist's relationships and morality, how they view themselves, and how they relate to the world.

However, while character arc-aligned power escalation has its benefits, it will not fit every story. Extremely hard power systems tend to stay away from aligning with character arcs because emotions and character traits are not strictly definable or predictable in the way that hard power systems depend on for setup and payoff. If handled badly, the escalation can amount to trope-ish scenarios where our wizard Graham succeeds because of the power of friendship or getting angrier and yelling louder than his opponent.[10]

It is a more useful technique for softer power systems. If you wish to have a power system where the only factor is how creative and intelligent a character is in using it, then incorporating character elements risks undermining the dramatic tension you are aiming for. Despite saying that it can give extra emotional weight to story beats, there is plenty to be said for letting story beats stand on their own. Letting characters resolve their personal issues in down-to-earth, introspective scenes is impactful without flashy magic powerups to manifest that change.

<u>Escalation and tension</u>

It is almost universally true in science fiction and fantasy that as powers escalate, so does the tension. Bigger stakes, grander acts, more dangerous villains as the story progresses for Graham. This is not to say this is a pattern you *should* follow, but it is to say this tends to happen.

Consider Lev Grossman's *Magician* series: the first book has Quentin and the other characters using moderate magical abilities to take down the Beast, a creature killing students, the second book scales up the stakes and their powers as they face old gods who have returned to get rid of magic, and the third does this yet again, scaling up the stakes and their powers with the entirety of the magical world about to be destroyed. Each time, the characters must learn bigger and more fantastical spells to resolve the plot. By the third, they are literally recreating the magical world.

Part of this is for novelty. Authors do not want to tell the same story each time, and one way to alter the type of story you are telling is upping or lowering the stakes, darkening or lightening the tone, or changing the scale of the story—both in

---

[10] Here's looking at you *Dragonball Z.*

terms of the setting and the powers. This is partly why it is so common for a first story to be set in a single location and later stories involve the characters venturing outside that place. Escalating powers is just one sliding scale that authors use to bring variety.

Some writers fall into a trap of thinking that because either each story in a series or the arc of a single book is continually bigger, bolder, better, stronger, faster—*more*—with continually grander displays of the power system, that it will be more exciting and emotionally compelling.

This is not true.

It is not necessarily something people consciously believe, but it is an underlying temptation that is hard to recognise in our writing and avoid because growing in scale is not inherently a bad thing.

When it is a bad thing, it is called power creep: when power escalation eclipses story.

One symptom of power creep is exponentially growing stakes to match power escalation without those stakes becoming more meaningful. Book one is saving a family, book two is saving a city, book three is saving the entire galaxy and the multiverse while we are at it. At some point readers just stop caring because we have no real grasp of that kind of scale. This is especially the case if this kind of scale is used repeatedly, which continual power escalations tends to lead to. You will remember television shows from when you were a kid that continually promised that the whole world was at stake every single time. What are you doing to make those larger stakes or powers more meaningful?

In Eoin Colfer's *Artemis Fowl and the Last Guardian*, the possible loss of Butler, a character we have known for eight books, carries more weight than the possibility of the world ending. It is simply far closer to our emotional investment in the story. Part of the reason *Artemis Fowl and the Opal Deception* stands as one of the best in the series is not that we see cooler gadgets and powers, but that it narrows in on the more personal stakes: the loss of close friends in their efforts to stop the villain. It makes those stakes, however large, personally meaningful to the reader and character.

If the reader's experience is dominated by incredible powers and high stakes with nothing to ground it in an emotional journey, then the story becomes spectacle. Consider what your reader is primarily experiencing when you raise the stakes and escalate powers.

Power creep can also undermine immersion. There is a lot of power escalation in Sanderson's *Mistborn* series, but it never loses the foundational rules and framework that made it unique and immersive in *The Final Empire*: skilled people doing very smart things with the Allomantic magic system. That was what drew readers initially and it was what kept them reading to the end.

In contrast, shonen anime like *Naruto* are often criticised for losing what made their original stories unique and immersive. Characters begin as strategic martial artists and end up shooting energy blasts into the moon. The ninja element at the core of the story at the beginning drops away. It is almost like people continue to follow the story *despite* the powers rather than because of them.

Where expansions on Sanderson's Allomantic powers always felt possible within the world from the beginning, steep power escalation risks losing some of the nuances of the original power system for the sake of grander abilities, either breaking or bending the rules beyond what readers want.

Power ceilings

Power ceilings establish a limit for the power system early on. Raymond E Feist's *Riftwar Saga* features massive power escalation across the series. The first book starts out with fireballs and lightning bolts, and the final books go on to fighting godlike beings with godlike powers. Planets can be destroyed, portals can be created with the blink of an eye, and a single wizard can bring the whole sky down on you. Yet, this works because Feist established a power ceiling with Macros the Black in the first book: a wizard so powerful he is suggested to be capable of all these things. The reader then has the expectation that Pug might one day reach that point too.

In terms of reader experience, power ceilings help powers feel earned because it means they do not come out of nowhere. An antagonist turning out more powerful and dangerous than we could have ever imagined is a lot less of an issue, like a puzzle being more complex than we ever thought it would be, but protagonists solving problems with unexpected powers runs into issues. It robs the story of a sense of predictability and consistency that makes watching them solve problems satisfying. For more information, check out *On Writing and Worldbuilding Volume I,* where we discuss hard and soft magic systems in more detail.

It is worth noting that this is an idea heavily refracted through a western lens. Our stories tend to place a lot of emphasis on this specific kind of predictability. The JRPG genre and magical realism often subvert these ideas with radical, unexpected, but thematically cogent powers. Sometimes, breaking the power ceiling is thematically important.

This leaves us with a question: how do you maintain or continue building tension when you do not want the power system to escalate anymore?

Incomparables

Perhaps you want your character to be as powerful as they can be by part way through the book or series. In Ursula Le Guin's *A Wizard of Earthsea,* Ged reaches his peak by the end of the second act. You might reasonably assume that powers need to escalate until the highest point of tension in the story. Otherwise, they would be powerful enough to resolve the plot, right? Villain two must be more powerful than villain one, and villain three must be more powerful than villain two *ad infinitum*.

It is an intuitive idea, easy to believe, but it is not true.

The first way to deal with this is with incomparable powers. Incomparables are abilities that do not work on the same scale. In Marvel's *Jessica Jones* series, the protagonist has super strength. In the first series, Jones must face down against Kilgrave, a man who can force others to do anything with just his voice. In the third season, the antagonist is Gregory Sallinger, a serial killer. He does not even have powers, but he is cunning, smart, and manipulative. Mind control and intelligence cannot be measured against strength in any meaningful way. The tension dynamic and obstacles to taking down someone who can control others is vastly different to taking down a serial killer with the law on his side.

Despite no power escalation, with Jones being about as powerful as she ever gets from the first season, tension is steadily maintained because the obstacles our hero faces are incomparable. Even if she did get stronger, beating Kilgrave would not equip her for beating Sallinger. They each pose a different challenge to Jessica Jones.

The key is that each villain [1] requires Jones to be smarter in different ways, and [2] challenges her morally in different ways. Perhaps Graham could be pitted against a character who is entirely invulnerable to any of his abilities in the first book. Then he must go up against a witch he loved when he was younger. Then in the third, his enemy is a queen who comes back every time she dies.

Patrick Rothfuss is the author of the *The Kingkiller Chronicles*, and in discussing how to handle power creep he said:

> 'Kvothe learns things and becomes slightly more
> powerful, but he solves all of his problems not
> through the application of power, but because he's

clever… If you are clever once, you have to be
clever again—there's constant tension.'[11]

Attaining power alone will not defeat the antagonist.
However, this is a cold and calculating method that does not add
any emotional or character dimensions to the conflict. While it
makes the conflict feel fresh and novel, it does not make it
emotionally compelling. This leads on to a second way to deal
with this.

Character challenges

Antagonists who challenge the protagonist on a personal
or moral level are another way to solve this problem. To
continue with Ged in *A Wizard of Earthsea*, though he reaches the
height of his power just halfway through the book, his ultimate
enemy is a ghostlike specter that haunts and follows him. No
amount of fire can kill it; no amount of magic can banish it. It is
only by confronting his darker impulses and accepting that he
has responsibilities to face up to that he can defeat this shadowy
creature. The antagonist was ultimately a challenge to his
worldview and morality.

One of the advantages to this is that when an antagonist
truly challenges the character on a personal level, you do not
need high stakes or spectacle to make it tense. The poster boy for
this idea is *The Dark Knight* and the Joker. Despite being the film
with technically the lowest stakes—two boatloads of people
compared to the entire city of Gotham—it is undeniably the most
tense and compelling of the trilogy. It challenges Batman to ask
how far he is willing to go to stop the Joker, which principles he
will abandon, and which ones he will cling to when the chips are
down.

When considering what makes your antagonist a threat, do
not just think about their powers, but how they fit in with your

---

[11] Patrick Rothfuss "Power Creep" (JoJo Cruise 2017, San Diego)

protagonist's morality, flaws, and biases. What is it about them that will turn them into more of a challenge than they otherwise would have been to anyone else. Sometimes, the most terrifying villain is the one who, without powers of their own, can make the protagonist feel utterly powerless.

These techniques also work for overpowered characters or stories about people whose powers do not escalate at all. Handling power escalation is difficult, but in the end it is more about allowing the story to grow organically without it losing anything to spectacle.

Summary

1. One way to escalate power systems logically and believably while making powers feel earned is with character arc-aligned power systems. This helps with narrative cohesion by tying internal and external conflicts together. However, it is less suited to hard magic systems.
2. It is natural for power systems to escalate as the tension rises throughout a book or series. However, continual escalation can become power creep, which in turn undermines narrative tension by losing immersive elements or creating a lack of meaningful and believable stakes.
3. Power ceilings help powers feel earned and help set up expectations for the reader. They are more relevant to protagonists than antagonists.
4. One way to maintain tension without power escalation is through incomparable abilities, meaning becoming more powerful will not necessarily resolve the plot.
5. A second way to maintain tension without power escalation is through character challenges: when antagonists challenge the protagonist on a personal level, and the tension is derived from difficult moral choices they are forced to make.

FLASHBACKS AND BACKSTORY

The Great Gatsby by F Scott Fitzgerald
The Three Body Problem by Cixin Liu
A Song of Ice and Fire by GRR Martin
Paper Towns by John Green
The Fault in Our Stars by John Green
Harry Potter and the Deathly Hallows by JK Rowling
Harry Potter and the Half-Blood Prince by JK Rowling
Avatar: The Last Airbender by Mike DiMartino and Bryan Konietzko
The Last Time We Say Goodbye by Cynthia Hand
Eleanor and Park by Rainbow Rowell
Story of Your Life by Ted Chiang
Madeline by Amal El-Mohtar

In our previous chapter on pacing, we discussed the Sidequest Problem: where obstacles in the plot may extend the story but ultimately do not contribute to narrative payoff, consequently grinding the story's pacing to a halt. Flashbacks often create a similar pacing problem because the reader is forced to step away from the core narrative that they are invested in—what is called the front story—to instead learn about what may be a very separate story that is only tenuously related, or related in a way not yet revealed, with stakes that they may not care about. This is not always the case, but the most important question to ask is whether you really need them.

Should the flashback be included at all?

A common mistake is thinking that because a character has a backstory, it must be communicated. This is not true. The skill is knowing which stuff to keep and which to summarise or leave out. Characters can have lives and stories outside of your novel without that needing to be explicitly communicated. It can inform their decisions and character.

In F Scott Fitzgerald's *The Great Gatsby*, Gatsby is desperately in love with Daisy, who is married to another man when he finally reconnects with her, and all the wealth he has made is to win her over. In a flashback as detailed as any other dramatic scene in the book, Fitzgerald takes the time to recount how Gatsby thought himself worthless when he met her as a 'penniless man without a past'. The flashback details the passionate time they spent together when they were younger.

Fitzgerald works to show us what is sometimes called the 'ghost': the source of the moral and psychological struggles of a character. The flashback not only exposes Gatsby's flaw—believing that wealth is his worth—but it also adds tension, depth, and understanding to the events of the front story as, now a rich man, he pursues Daisy. We see why he wants her so much and the history the two characters share.

You may conclude from this that any defining moment from a character's past should be included, but that is not the case. The distinction is in the backstory's relevance to the narrative, and not all events that drastically impact a character necessarily impact the narrative directly. While this backstory helps us understand why Gatsby is the way he is in the front story, its more important role is contextualising Gatsby's reckless pursuit of Daisy that ultimately culminates in his death. One of the major themes in the story is about the failure of the American Dream: rags to riches. This flashback is crucial to understanding that, showing not only how deeply tied his wealth is to his view of himself but also to his view of Daisy as a prize to be won. It also more deeply develops that toxic connection between wealth and happiness — something Gatsby believes but will ultimately be proved hollow. Gatsby's traumatic experiences during the First World War almost definitely shaped the person he became, but Fitzgerald chose not to include any flashbacks that focused on that because he understood it would not inform the choices Gatsby is making in the front story, helping us understand his flaws that generate the conflict.

Flashbacks can develop tension, letting us see *why* a character cares so much about the goal, what they believe is at stake, understanding where the Lie they believe comes from — about the world or themselves. Author Mary Robinette Kowal built on this in saying:

> 'When flashbacks work well, they are adding to the forward momentum of the story by giving the reader the information they need to understand the… context of what's at stake.'

Margaret Atwood's *The Testaments* makes extensive use of flashbacks to Aunt Lydia's past to explore how ruthless she needed to be to survive the rise of Gilead, the indignities she suffered in the process, the temptation to hurt others in the name of righteousness, and from that why she cares so much about bringing it down. It also shows us where her flawed, utilitarian and unempathetic worldview comes from — the Lie she believes. Flashbacks can develop the theme, giving us a deeper understanding of the meaning behind the story.

Flashbacks can also reveal something that complicates the front story, recontextualising information the reader already has. In Cixin Liu's *The Three Body Problem*, part of the story flashes back to events that transpired at a secret military base in China dedicated to contacting alien life. As the front story protagonist slowly pieces together what the strange simulation game he was invited to play means, the flashback complicates our understanding of the story. The game simulates the alien world of Trisolaris, the home of an alien species that found Earth through transmissions from that secret military base all those years ago. The Trisolarans are already coming for Earth because a person at that base welcomed them with hopes they would subdue humanity. Suddenly, the world is in a lot more danger than we ever thought, and the game is not a harmless maths problem, but a recruitment tool for a terrorist organisation hellbent on bringing humanity under the Trisolaran thumb.[12]

All of these enrich narrative payoff.

Flashbacks that just give readers more information about a character do not necessarily feel relevant to the front story and can risk slowing. Simply because a character has a tragic backstory does not mean it needs to be communicated in real time. There are also more efficient ways of explaining character motivation or getting readers to sympathise with characters that do not require them to step away from the story they are invested in. This is especially true considering that the importance of past events is often best demonstrated by showing how it affects the characters in the present.

Backstory, like a lot of worldbuilding, can be like an iceberg: the reader may only see the parts relevant to the story even if the author knows there is a lot more going on down there.

Personally, I feel that relevance to the narrative is a high bar. In my book, a main character has a traumatic backstory that is intimately relevant to the tension of the plot, but I chose not to write this out in flashback. The story is about dealing with trauma in the years after, and I want to develop empathy based on those experiences rather than from the traumatic events themselves. The only flashbacks I do include are to better understand the main character and build into the theme that

---

[12] It is not confirmed that the Trisolarans have thumbs. It is worth noting that *The Three Body Problem* arguably uses parallel stories rather than flashbacks. However, while the Red Coast story mostly stands on its own, it is clearly framed to recontextualise the events of the front story.

abuse is often invisible to those immediately around it. Still, on revision and feedback from beta readers, I cut these flashbacks down to their bare minimum because some readers felt they were slowing the pacing.

An exception

Despite my pontificating here, if you want to keep the flashbacks and backstory in, do it. Your story is your own and that you tell the story you want to tell is what is ultimately more important. The most 'efficient' way to do flashbacks may not be the way you wish to tell your story, and that is okay.

I suspect this is sometimes the case with GRR Martin's *A Song of Ice and Fire* series. In one book, Martin has a character walking through a hall, where he spots a series of tapestries that remind him of his exploits when he was younger, rescuing the king from capture almost singlehandedly. He then allows several pages for this tangent into the past, despite it adding little to the front story, and primarily just letting us know more about the character at hand.

It is also worth noting the difference between flashbacks and parallel stories. Though they may appear similar in some ways, parallel stories are often independent for a time before becoming connected later. The key is that flashbacks depend on a front story to be relevant or meaningful, whereas parallel stories mostly stand on their own.

The two kinds of flashback

How long and detailed should a flashback be? Flashbacks exist on a spectrum between half scenes and full scenes, and they each serve different narrative purposes.

Consider the opening to John Green's *Paper Towns,* where several years prior to the main narrative, Quentin and Margo find a dead body. This is a full scene flashback, written with all the sensory detail that any other part of the story has. It is 1500 words long, is not summarised, and is separated into its own chapter. This does two things:

1. It signals to the reader that this part of his backstory is particularly relevant to the front story in a way characters simply recounting the event might not.
2. The extra detail gives these moments more dramatic and emotional weight than a character summarising the event usually would.[13] It also introduces the key symbol of the 'strings' — 'Maybe all the strings inside him broke' — which plays a major role in Quentin's perception of the events that follow, as well as his understanding of Margo.

In contrast, consider this half scene flashback John Green uses in *The Fault in Our Stars* where Hazel recalls spending an afternoon with her father in a river:

> Even though it was a geographic inconvenience, I really liked Holliday Park. When I was a little kid, I would wade in the White River with my dad and there was always this great moment when he would throw me up in the air, just toss me away from him, and I would reach out my arms as I flew and he would reach out his arms, and then we would both see that our arms were not going to touch and no one was going to catch me, and it would kind of scare the shit out of both of us in the best possible way, and then I would legs-flailingly hit the water and then come up for air uninjured and the current would bring me back to him as I said again, Daddy, again.

---

[13] *On Writing and Worldbuilding Volume I* features a chapter on writing prologues, which intricately links in with this analysis. It discusses the introduction on the 'strings' metaphor.

This moment is briefly summarised in one-hundred-and-fifty words. It has very few lines of quoted dialogue that allow any conversation to play out. Half scenes are for less important moments that still give insight into characters without holding the dramatic or emotional weight or thematic context we expect from full flashbacks. They do not risk disrupting the pacing because they do not take the reader away from the front story.

Flashbacks do not need to be as long or short as these but figuring out which elements of backstory are important enough to be full scenes and which should be half scenes is up to you as a writer. How much less impactful would Snape's memories of Lily in *Harry Potter and the Deathly Hallows* be as a half scene instead of full scene, and how annoying would it be to get a full scene flashback every time Ron referenced something Fred and George did at home when he was younger?

<u>Making flashbacks work</u>

In *Harry Potter and the Half-Blood Prince,* Harry spends time persuading Professor Slughorn to tell him what he told Tom Riddle about making horcruxes—items that contain a piece of your soul. Slughorn gave Dumbledore a fake memory but eventually gives up the real one to Harry, and the story gives us a full scene flashback to the past. Even though the story is told from Harry's perspective, this is Slughorn's backstory. It works for a couple reasons:

1. Rowling takes a lot of page time to invest the reader in this mystery: what did Slughorn tell Riddle? The decision to give the reader fake memories multiple times before revealing the truth generates intrigue. It foreshadows what is to come. By making it a goal to uncover the truth in the front story, there is no risk of undermining the pacing—it *is* the front story even in a full flashback.

2. This flashback also actively moves the narrative forward. By this point in the story, the flashback is so intimately tied to the tension in the front story that it seamlessly moves the narrative into its third act by establishing new stakes: destroying a horcrux. It does not feel like the pacing has halted at all.

Fundamentally, some flashbacks work because though they step away from the front story chronologically, they stay with it in terms of narrative momentum. Consider giving your flashback some information that changes the story going forward, revealing a foreshadowed secret or introducing a new problem that characters were not yet aware of, changing the stakes or their understanding of what they are facing.

Scene structure

Some people say that you should not have flashbacks in the first few chapters or fifty pages, and as a broad guideline, that is fair. Forcing a reader away from the main story too quickly is jarring. This is why a lot of advice focuses on how to best segue into them—through a scene break, a dream, a triggered memory when a character sees something, or something else entirely. Personally though, I feel how you segue into it is a lot less important than where the flashback comes in your scene structure.

> 'One of the things that a non-linear narrative does for you is… it allows you to present the narrative pieces in the order that the audience needs for the maximum emotional impact.'
> — Mary Robinette Kowal[14]

---

[14] Brandon Sanderson, Amal El-Mohtar, Mary Robinette Kowal, Maurice Broaddus "Backstories" (podcast, 13 May 2018) Writing Excuses <writingexcuses.com>

Scene structure is less about chronology and more about controlling the order in which the reader experiences aspects of your story. A common structure used for flashback scenes is placing them so that they comment or give a deeper context to the front story scene either immediately before or immediately after.

In Mike DiMartino and Bryan Konietzko's *Avatar: The Last Airbender,* the episode *The Southern Air Temple* features several flashbacks to the protagonist's past growing up in a temple they are visiting in the episode. As Aang wanders through the ruins of his childhood home, we get the immediate contrast between what he remembers it to be like—full of life, colour, and laughter—and what the place is like now—a grim shadow of its former self. These flashbacks centre around Aang's relationship with Monk Gyatso, his mentor, only for them to be immediately followed by the discovery of Monk Gyatso's corpse in the front story.

The flashback here not only builds into the episode's tension as Aang slowly discovers that his people were the victims of genocide, but the structure of the reveal gives the front story beat extra dramatic and emotional context it would not otherwise carry. Endearing us to Gyatso and then revealing him to be dead takes us on Aang's emotional journey. Were we to simply find the body without seeing him as part of Aang's life, the discovery would not hit as hard.

In contrast, placing a flashback immediately after a story beat tends to work best when the author wants the reader begging for an explanation for why a character acted a certain way—rather than the author wanting you to feel what the character feels.

But we can take this to another level. As discussed in previous chapters, I personally find the active and reactive scene structure the most helpful. To reiterate our definition: the active scene involves a goal, a conflict, and a disaster/resolution while the reactive scene involves a reaction, a dilemma, and a decision. Because writing is complicated, the line between these scenes will often get blurred. Not every active or reactive scene will follow each of these beats in this order, and sometimes it is helpful to consider them as six beats within a single scene. Personally, I find this more helpful. But the point remains that flashbacks are often seamlessly incorporated into the reaction, dilemma, and decision beats.

In *The Last Time We Say Goodbye* by Cynthia Hand, Lex is struggling to stop blaming herself for the suicide of her brother. Hand starts out writing an active scene:

> GOAL: trying to stop another boy taking his own life.
> CONFLICT: she needs to break into his house somehow.
> SETBACK: she finds out her brother called this boy the night he died.

The reactive scene following this perfectly segues into a flashback of the night her brother died.

> REACTION: deep shock, confusion, an inability to parse how she feels about this new information.
> DILEMMA: how will she deal with this? By clinging to her guilt or accepting that her brother's suicide may be more complicated than she initially thought?
> DECISION: she processes her feelings by journaling her memory of the night he died. This then passes right into a detailed full scene flashback.

Flashbacks often detail the emotional makeup or explain the thinking of a character, meaning they naturally fit into the emotional reaction of a character, especially if something in the conflict or resolution relates to their past, or to their dilemma if it mirrors a choice they had to make previously, or as Cynthia Hand does—the decision.

I will mention that filter words like realised, noticed, remembered, and recalled remind the reader they are being told about a thing rather than shown. It is natural to lean on these verbs, but they can make a flashback less effective. Consider this passage in Rainbow Rowell's *Eleanor and Park*:

> But Park hadn't thought that either, the first time he saw Eleanor on the bus. He remembered thinking that it was bad enough that she looked the way she did… He remembered feeling embarrassed for her. And now… Now, he felt the fight rising up in his throat.

The filter words abstract the reader's experience from the beats of the flashback. Imagine if it were written like this:

> But Park hadn't thought that either, the first time he saw Eleanor on the bus. He thought it was bad enough that she looked the way she did. He felt embarrassed for her. And now… Now, there was a fight rising up in his throat.

There is no extra layer between the reader and the character's experiences.

Recontextualisation

In Ted Chiang's *Story of Your Life*, the narrative is repeatedly interrupted by a series of odd scenes. The film adaption, 2016's *Arrival*, depicts these scenes as flashbacks for the main character, but the short story depicts them more as a woman imagining her future daughter's life:

> And then there will be the times when I see you laughing. Like the time you'll be playing with the neighbor's puppy…
> 'But I'm not sleepy,' you'll whine…

What matters for our discussion is that these are non-linear scenes. In much the same way as a flashback, they take us out of the chronological narrative, and as you read them in the short story, they do not provide the extra context or weight to the front story you may be used to—until the end. It is revealed that these nonlinear scenes are flashforwards in time, not imaginings, because as the front story progresses, the main character develops the ability to see parts of the future—and she now knows that her future daughter is going to die young.

The front story entirely recontextualises these nonlinear scenes with a twist at the end. They suddenly take on a new meaning. Littering these scenes across the story was still crucial to the narrative payoff, it just was not immediate. To account for this, Ted Chiang employs a couple of techniques to keep the reader engaged. He writes these nonlinear scenes in second person present tense for the most part: 'You do this, you do that'. Though it reads like a woman imagining the future, it feels off. Not only would we usually read this kind of scene in past tense or future tense, but the woman suddenly imagines her daughter dying—something no hopeful mother would usually do. The reader immediately understands that there is something else going on here, even if we do not know what. Chiang subtly introduces a question that he answers at the end. If you are going to pepper backstory throughout the book, then this is a good model. Building a mystery around the non-linear scenes keeps them interesting.

Trauma

It is difficult to talk about flashbacks without addressing the context in which they are often used: traumatic experiences. They are effective as full scenes because they make clear how important this moment is to a character's emotional makeup and the detail affords the events more dramatic weight. However, there are a few things to consider.

In terms of developing reader empathy for your characters, trauma is just as much about how it affects a character now as it is about what happened all those years ago. It is even arguably more effective to focus on those long-term consequences. The things that they are afraid of or find hard because of those experiences. Simply knowing something bad happened to someone in the past does not generate the same sympathy as seeing how deeply it affects them to this day. In discussing the traumatic flashbacks used in her short story *Madeline*, Amal El-Mohtar said:

> 'What I [wanted to do] was to really dive deep into the sensory effects of the story, so that you could get a sense of what it would be like to just have this really dislocating and terrifying thing happen to you.'[15]

Flashbacks are not just a narrative device to look back on the past. They are a visceral emotional and psychological experience. Flashbacks and PTSD are intensely difficult experiences and allowing the reader to see what it is like to be dragged back to that horrible moment can be enlightening.

Summary

1. Like worldbuilding, not all backstory needs to be communicated. A good test is whether it is relevant to the narrative—helping recontextualise the front story, or to develop the tension, core themes, or our understanding of character decisions. This is often through showing the character's 'ghost'.
2. Flashbacks can be written as half scenes or full scenes. The greater the narrative importance, dramatic and emotional weight, and insight into character a backstory moment has, the more detail you can justify. Keep in mind how it affects your pacing.

---

[15] Brandon Sanderson, Amal El-Mohtar, Mary Robinette Kowal, Maurice Broaddus "Backstories" (podcast, 13 May 2018) Writing Excuses <writingexcuses.com>

3. Flashbacks are often made more effective by generating intrigue and mystery, and then allowing the flashback to give answers. One way to avoid pacing issues is to use them to move the story forward by establishing new stakes, introducing a new problem, or changing a character's position in the story—altering how the story works going forward.

4. Carefully structure where your flashbacks go to maximise impact. This is often done by using a flashback scene to comment on the front story beat immediately before or after, or by connecting it to the reaction, the dilemma, or the decision in a reactive scene.

5. Filter words can make flashbacks less immersive. These are words like, 'remembered', 'felt', and 'recalled'.

6. Flashbacks can be used to explore trauma, but the experience of trauma is often just as much about how it affects characters now as it is about what happened in the past.

WRITING CIVIL WARS

All Quiet on the Western Front by Erich Maria Remarque
A Farewell to Arms by Ernest Hemingway
Two Brothers, One North, One South by Walt Whitman
Ten Days That Shook the World by John Reed
Captain America: Civil War directed by Anthony Russo and Joe Russo
Purgatory Mount by Adam Roberts
The Legend of Korra created by Mike DiMartino and Bryan Konietzko
A Game of Thrones by GRR Martin
Cold Mountain by Charles Frazier
Snow Crash by Neal Stephenson

With brothers killing brothers, interpersonal drama, and political intrigue, it is no surprise the civil war is such a popular fictional premise. Civil wars range from small-scale skirmishes to the widespread, systematic fracturing of a state into a dozen different factions, and to discuss how they might fit into your story, we are going to break them down into five parts: tension and national identity, three realistic factors in causing civil war, character arcs, the first act, and the tragedy of the setting.

Tension and national identity

This might come as a surprise, but World War I was not very good. So not very good, in fact, that in the decades after the conflict, a whole lot of young men went home and started writing about just how not very good it really was. They gave us

famous stories like *All Quiet on the Western Front* by Erich
Maria Remarque and *A Farewell to Arms* by Ernest Hemingway.
If large-scale modern warfare sparked 'war is miserable' stories,
then civil war sparked the 'brother kills brother' stories we are so
familiar with like Walt Whitman's *Two Brothers, One North, One
South,* which tells the tale of two brothers fighting on opposite
sides during the American Civil War.

War stories can position characters on opposing sides, but
the setting of a civil war puts a unique spotlight on families and
friends within the same community being divided, exploring
how different groups of people believe the same country and
people should live and work. John Reed's *Ten Days That Shook
the World* recounts the turmoil in early twentieth century Russia
as more an ideological battle of national identity than anything
else—of the place of monarchy, rights, and political freedoms.
Captain America: Civil War positioned old friends Tony Stark and
Steve Rodgers on strictly different ideological sides of the
Sokovia Accords, using the fracturing of this relationship as the
central tension in the story. Such schisms are ripe with
interpersonal drama.

Plenty of stories feature civil wars without using this
dramatic setup. *Purgatory Mount* by Adam Roberts tells the story
of a group of friends caught up in the powers that be during a
second American Civil War. It is a setting, and these are still
'civil war stories', but they are not what we will be discussing in
this chapter. We will focus on stories that explore ideas under
the guise of character conflict.

Characters may struggle over their allegiance,
relationships, and ideals as they are forced to not only pick a side
but to whom they are loyal. They struggle not just with
competing ideas of the nation but with competing ideas of the
self. *The Legend of Korra* does this surprisingly well. When a civil
war breaks out between the Northern and Southern Water
Tribes, Korra must choose between her loyalty to her home and
family, the South, and her duty to the spirits as the Avatar, more
in line with the North. Korra goes back and forth between

refusing to intervene to help the South and threatening a judge to defend her family. Behind all this looms questions of sovereignty, unity, and the place of spirituality in a newly emerging Southern culture.

Importantly, though this civil war story deals with abstract concepts, we become invested in the struggle through Korra. Neal Stephenson can take a fifty-page tangent to discuss Sumerian history and the coding of the human mind in *Snow Crash*, but most of the time, the reader becomes invested in these ideas through how characters interact with them. They feel betrayed by their friends, feel hatred for their neighbours, anxiety over their traditional way of life being uprooted, frustration that others could believe such terrible things, and turmoil over the pull in a new and more terrifying ideological direction.

<u>Three realistic factors in civil war</u>

Realism is worth discussing because it matters to a lot of writers, especially when worldbuilding. This is not intended as an exhaustive list, so just treat these as prompts rather than rules. These elements may play into the conflict between your characters.

In 2004, economists Collier and Hoeffler summarised that:

> '[Ideological] grievances are immaterial because they are [constants in civil war]... According to this microeconomic framework, civil wars can be expected to break out where opportunity costs of fighting are low because of poverty, and where wartime gains stemming from looting natural resources lead to... enrichment.'[16]

---

[16] *The Dynamics and Logics of Civil War,* Lars-Erik Cederman, Manuel Vogt, 2017, Journal of Conflict Resolution

Essentially, they argued that grievance motivations like political inequality or injustice with a principled belief in getting rid of billionaires with a democratic guillotine to the neck are less important causes of civil war than a socio-political environment that is low risk and high return for starting a civil war. That you will get a lot out of it without much to lose. If that is the case, then an ideology will spring up around it to give armed insurrection some framing.

We see this play out in the 1918-1922 Russian Civil War. While there were ideologies at play—capitalism, communism, and monarchism—there was a lot to be gained economically and politically for the working class and not a lot to lose. Living standards in Russia were some of the lowest in Europe at the time with serfdom only being abolished in 1861. The Reds, having just taken control of the country, had a lot to lose is they could not establish a stable rule. Grievance did still play a role. To pretend that Lenin's passionate opposition to working class injustices did nothing would be fallacious, but he was equally a galvanising force at the right time in the right place. Grievances alone can be remedied in a stable and economically viable state with institutions to address them, but Russia at the time lacked that flexibility.

Secondly, stability. Statistically, civil wars break out more often in states that are already unstable, following on from the low risk, high returns model. The First Roman Civil War saw the dispossessed poor flood into Rome, creating instability and leading to conflicts between the Populares like Gaius Marius and Optimates like Sulla. These tensions resulted in the obliteration of the Roman constitution with people holding consul positions beyond legal limits. All this further increased instability and it culminated in a civil war.

Instability is also often due to a breakdown in the capacity of established systems to deal with conflict, grievances, and injustices. A 2004 paper highlights that a state's instability is hallmarked by an inability of opposing factions to believe the other faction can act in good faith:

'The problem when it comes to institutional choices is that there is no such impartial third party that can be trusted to enforce contracts. This is the origin of the commitment problem in politics.'[17]

In 1891, the Chilean Civil War sparked after a breakdown in relations between the Office of the President and Congress. They each refused to entertain the other's initiatives. With the gears of politics grinding to a halt, many felt the only way to get them moving again was violence.

The role of violence in affecting someone's allegiance is worth considering. It is easy to think people would join a side for wholly ideological reasons. The optimistic angle of fantastical revolutionary stories leads us to feel we would pick the side that believes the 'right' things. The reality is that studies on the relationship between violence and allegiance revealed that civilians reacted to indiscriminate violence in their region or home by colluding with the perpetrators' adversary.[18] Though many will join a side for ideological reasons or perhaps personal gain, proximity to violence and war crimes and who perpetrated them will more viscerally shape how a person views each side, regardless of what they stand for. Ideology is hard to parse during war when both sides mostly see you down the barrel of a gun. This is the human brain being irrational but very human. If we see one side targeting our home, our friends, or our pet cat Momo, even accidentally, then we are far more likely to join their adversary because it just becomes personal.

The war in Afghanistan from 2001 onward has had the unfortunate consequence of inflating terrorist groups, not because they necessarily agree with their extreme Islamist

---

[17] *Institutions as the fundamental cause of long-run growth*, Acemoglu, Johnson, Robinson, 2004, National Bureau of Economic Research
[18] Sebastian Schutte 'Violence and Civilian Loyalties: Evidence from Afghanistan' (2017) Journal of Conflict Resolution, DOI: 10.1177/0022002715626249.

values, but because civilians saw western nations bombing their homes and killing their children more than they saw these terrorist groups doing the same. One study showed that the 1955-1975 Vietnam Civil War saw civilians joining the Vietcong when bombed nearby by the United States.[19] Ideological concerns were entirely secondary.

<u>Character arcs</u>

Stories revel in the conflict between what a character wants and what they need. A character might think they want the adoration of millions but truly need the love of their family. Civil wars set the stage for characters to want glory, or power, or wealth, or a Great Perhaps, but to truly need stability, companionship, love, and humility. In GRR Martin's *A Song of Ice and Fire*, Ser Jorah was initially sent to spy on or even kill a rival during a potential civil war: Daenerys, the Mother of Dragons. He does this in hope of earning a royal pardon and returning from exile to Westeros. As the story progresses however, he joins Daenerys and gives up on this chance of being legitimised again. This is a major point of development for him in *A Game of Thrones*. The civil war framed Jorah's internal conflict. Doing what he believed to be right meant letting go of what he wanted and discovering what he truly needed: a purpose in a righteous fight.

This violence factor naturally lends itself to impactful scenes and arcs in a civil war story. Perhaps your protagonist's home is burned to the ground by the supposed 'good' guys and she is taken in by the fascists. Disillusionment and growth are sure to follow. GRR Martin used this with the Karstarks during the War of Five Kings in *A Song of Ice and Fire*. House Karstark first felt they were fighting to protect the North, but after King

---

[19] Kocher, Matthew Adam, Thomas B Pepinsky, Stathis N. Kalyvas, 'Aerial Bombing and Counterinsurgency in the Vietnam War' (2011) American Journal of Political Science 55 (2)

Robb executed Lord Karstark for treason, they abandoned the fight entirely—a decision that contributed to Robb's ultimate demise. If you are going for a realistic civil war, then rather than asking what characters *believe,* ask what they would *feel* and to whom those feelings would guide them.

However, what characters want, believe, or feel may be entirely irrelevant. Up until the last century, people were mostly conscripted into armies. Perhaps your fictional world does not use conscription, but our world did. In Charles Frazier's *Cold Mountain*, Inman is fighting for the Confederates during the American Civil War against his will. This becomes a great source of personal conflict and growth—it is not simply that Inman does not believe in the cause he is forced to fight for; he is in fact passionately opposed to it.

The first act

In the first act of *Purgatory Mount,* Adam Roberts spends a significant time detailing the socioeconomic instability within the United States. It is crucial for creating a tense atmosphere where it feels like the fabric of orderly society is being held together by a tenuous string. It gives the story a sombre tone because so much is on the verge of being lost. You continually feel like the United States is a tinderbox and everyone has a match.

However, what is notable about *Purgatory Mount* is the way Roberts communicates all this. When writing a story leading up to a civil war, it is difficult to convey big concepts like economic downturn, political turmoil, and social breakdown when not writing from the perspectives of major military, political, or economic figures. Those perspectives are also often less familiar to the average reader.

Roberts writes from the perspective of Ottoline Barragão, a sixteen-year-old girl who likes bees. As he tells her story, he writes about how she now sees monolithic police towers that loom in the shape of an ever-increasing surveillance state, she meets hordes of homeless veterans and feels hopeless knowing she cannot help them, and her bees no longer produce sweet honey after the environment has collapsed. The honey is instead plain and tastes of plastic. Roberts lets us view these more abstract sociological problems through the lens of Ottoline's day-to-day experiences. We do not need to see employment statistics and political gridlock when the fixtures of ordinary life are melting away.

This helps establish setting and mood in a grounded way. Is bread suddenly too expensive to buy, do characters suffer a panic attack when all their plants start to die, and what do the children do when teachers do not turn up to school because they have not been paid? Using a couple of scenes to explore the grounded and personal effects the wider instability has on your characters gives the reader a world ripe for civil war more than seeing politicians argue or newspaper titles about plummeting stock markets ever will. Not only are those a lot lazier, but they are less relatable. Concrete details from your characters' lives are more relatable, and the more desperate your characters become, the more desperate the tone of your writing.

The tragedy of the setting

There has always been this myth about war being a glorious adventure. Civil wars have never quite attracted the same glossy image. They take place in your homeland, the bombs go off in your city, and the guillotine falls on the necks of your friends. In Charles Frazier's *Cold Mountain*, the American Civil War is shown to be uniquely destructive in the sense that both sides know that in the end, whoever wins, the country will still have lost thousands of lives and will be left with a shattered national identity. Unlike German soldiers taking French farms, the Union soldiers are taking the livelihoods of their fellow countrymen.

A lot of dramatic or emotional story beats can be derived from showing the effect of the civil war on places that characters are personally connected to. Perhaps they are forced to sack the town they were born in or they find their favourite romantic spot desecrated with bodies. Consider utilising that closeness to the destruction.

Summary

1. Civil war stories are equipped to derive tension from ideological and interpersonal conflict over national and personal identity. Though civil war stories may address abstract ideas, the reader becomes invested in these through characters interacting with them.
2. Realism can help in crafting a convincing setting. Civil wars spark when there is a lot to gain and not a lot to lose and a period of instability where traditional problem-solving institutions are ineffective. Who perpetrates violence where is a large determining factor in who joins which side.
3. Connecting the broader conflict of the civil war to character arcs may help the story feel more cohesive by bringing together character struggles and setting.
4. If writing a story that leads up to a civil war, consider intensifying everyday economic and social struggles to communicate the instability that sets the stage for your story. It will also humanise your characters.
5. Civil wars can bring the conflict closer to home. Weaving in your characters' homes or past can be a really good source of character conflict, pain, and shock.

WRITING IN FIRST PERSON

Twilight by Stephanie Meyer
The Hate U Give by Angie Thomas
The Woman in the Window by AJ Finn
Skyward by Brandon Sanderson
The Handmaid's Tale by Margaret Atwood
Parable of the Sower by Octavia E Butler
The Knife of Never Letting Go by Patrick Ness
The Hunger Games by Suzanne Collins
What Remains of Edith Finch developed by Giant Sparrow
The Last Time We Say Goodbye by Cynthia Hand

Twilight is a 2005 first-person novel by Stephenie Meyer written from the perspective of Bella Swan, an ordinary girl that finds herself in the midst of vampires, werewolves, and vitamin D deficient Cedric Diggory. It is almost universally used as a punching bag for writers everywhere, but as a fun exercise, we will be taking a genuine close look at the first-person writing of *Twilight* to see where it works, and where it does not. First-person writing is writing from inside the mind of a character, using the pronouns 'I' or 'We'. For example:

> I dove into a rose bush… We were ten, we didn't know what happened after you died. Hell, I still don't know.
> — *The Hate U Give,* Angie Thomas

In this chapter, we will discuss psychic distance, developing character voice, soft magic systems, the unreliable narrator, use of language, the difference factor, inference, confiding in the reader, and the first-person medium.

Psychic Distance

First-person writing means getting deep inside the mind of a character in a way you really cannot in third person. It gives the reader the closest psychic distance to the character, letting them engage with them in a uniquely intimate way. A first-person perspective is particularly well equipped for deeply psychological stories like AJ Finn's *The Woman in the Window*—a story about an agoraphobic woman, Anna Fox, whose perception of reality and self is continually called into question after she witnesses a murder, and then supposedly meets the very victim she saw die. The limited perspective means the reader's understanding of the world is limited by Anna's. Her fears are our own. Her psychological state is our own. AJ Finn wanted the reader to be as closely aligned with Anna Fox as possible. Any mistakes she makes in remembering or interpreting the world and people around her are seamlessly incorporated into our own experience.

The disadvantage to using the first-person perspective is that you give up the ability to describe scenes and places however you like. You are limited to the lens of your perspective character and describing the things the way they would. However, a strong character voice can make this account of people and the world even more compelling. Consider this description of a tunnel in Brandon Sanderson's *Skyward*:

> A lot of the rocks in the tunnel were broken and cracked, most likely from Krell bombings... I imagined those rocks as the broken bodies of my enemies, their bones shattered, their trembling arms reaching up in a useless gesture of total and complete defeat.

This passage bleeds with character, telling us how the caverns looked while also characterising Spensa. It tells us she has an active imagination, a fixation on this eternal battle her people are fighting, that she is not just okay with violence but revels in it. She wants to be a hero. All of this is proved true in later chapters. The description is not as complicated or poetic as it might be in third person, but it is just as vivid and even more full of character.

Filter words create psychic distance between the character and the reader, reminding the reader they are being told a story and therefore risking lifting them out of it. Filter words include 'imagined', 'saw', 'felt', and 'touched'. Consider this passage from *Twilight*:

> I felt Emmett stiffen next to me, and I wondered at his reaction to the word. It meant something more to the three of them…

Now, let us rephrase it without filter words:

> Emmett stiffened next to me, a strange reaction to the word. It meant something more to the three of them…

By removing the filter words, we feel more like we are there with Bella, and the sentences carry more of a punch. We do not need Bella to tell us she wondered about Emmett's reaction—it is implied in the language she uses to express her opinion about it.

In first person, 'I' is the dominant pronoun, but using it too much can be jarring and repetitive. So, remove it and rely on the *implied 'I'*. You could write:

> After I brushed my teeth, I worked to straighten out the tangled chaos of my hair. I splashed my face with cold water…

But by using the implied 'I', it becomes:

After brushing my teeth, I splashed my face with cold water and worked to straighten out the tangled chaos of my hair.

The sentence flows smoothly. We are immersed in the action rather than being constantly reminded who is performing it.

Developing a strong character voice

Developing a strong character voice is not as simple as having an interesting character. It is about allowing their character to inform the way you write the story. Margaret Atwood tells *The Handmaid's Tale* from the perspective of Offred, a handmaid in the Republic of Gilead. Handmaids are women systematically forced to birth children for the leaders of Gilead against their will. It is a grim, torturous life where there is little to enjoy. As a result, she continually recalls the past when describing the world around her:

We slept in what had once been the gymnasium… for the games that were formerly played there…

I look up at the ceiling, tracing the foliage of the wreath. Today it makes me think of a hat [that] women used to wear at some period during the old days…

Describing things in the present by comparing them to her past life shows us someone longing for the past, wishing they were there, reflecting on all the things they never appreciated before they were taken away.

Part of a strong character voice is figuring out what your perspective character would focus on or notice more. What do they care about or miss when describing a place or a person? When creating your character, consider giving them quirks, flaws, or insights that make their personal perspective compelling. A scientist who points out facts about the natural world. A psychopath who can read the people around him perfectly. A victim of abuse who often views those around him as threats. For a lot of people, these are unfamiliar perspectives — ways of looking at the world that we find interesting to experience.

Offred is a passive protagonist who regrets not acting before and finds herself largely unable to do so now; it is natural that her narration would dwell on the past. She is not prone to rebellion, so her descriptive focus is not usually on threats or escape routes. She almost never describes the war she hears about occasionally. It seems to barely register in her way of looking at the world.

We can contrast this with Spensa in Sanderson's *Skyward*. As an active character, a fighter, and someone who sees everyone around her as competition or a threat, her descriptions focus on those things. We read every detail she learns about the fights she sees, and she frames how others move and talk to her in ways that suggest they are a threat.

Find biases that will frame your character's storytelling. In any given scene, find something they might focus on, something they might miss, or something they might summarise instead of detailing. Offred might focus on what something reminds her of from before Gilead's existence while Spensa might miss when someone was kind to her.

Language, sentence structure, and word choice are important parts of developing a character voice. Characters will use particular words, phrases, and analogies to describe things based on who they are and what is important to them. To continue with our *Skyward* example, Spensa sometimes uses language that draws on legends and mythology — 'Every great warrior knew when they were bested' — or battlefields — 'I imagined those broken rocks as the broken bodies of my enemies'.

In Octavia E Butler's *Parable of the Sower,* Lauren Oya Olamina is tired of the constant struggle to survive in her apocalyptic world. Her home is continually vandalised, and she has been forced to grow up quicker than a teenager like her should have to. She views herself as a realist; someone with no illusions about her situation or the wider world. To capture this worldview, Butler minimises poeticisms, flowery language, and creative similes and metaphors. Lauren's language is grounded, focused on being realistic, clear, almost scornful at times:

> 'The husband of the woman had thrown off his attacker, and the two coyotes, finding themselves outnumbered, scampered away. Skinny, scared little bastards out to do their daily stealing.'

Language can indicate class, age, and setting as well. In Patrick Ness' *The Knife of Never Letting Go*, not only are longer words like 'education' spelled incorrectly, but he uses simpler descriptions, with the structure of his sentences tending to be simpler to remind us that the character whose voice he's writing in, Todd Hewitt, never received a full education, which is also a source of insecurity for him. Charles Dickens' characters constantly use language that indicates whether they are from the upper or lower classes. Lower class characters will slur or shorten their words and use titles like 'sir' or 'ma'am' after a life of having their place in society impressed upon them.

Find words or phrases your character will use more often, and more importantly, analogies, metaphors, and similes that they might use to tell their story. What are their points of reference? The weather? Shakespeare's plays? Science?

With all this in mind, it is worth considering why Bella Swan is considered a relatively flat first-person perspective in Stephenie Meyer's *Twilight*. Unlike Spensa, Todd Hewitt, Offred, or Lauren, Bella rarely uses language that defines her character. She does not seem to have any vocabulary, analogies, or metaphors that draw on her flaws, biases, desires, and needs. There is not a strong sense of subjectivity to her narration. Bella's perspective focuses on what moves the plot forward. In other words, she does not have a strong character voice, and it shows.

There is never a strong feeling that she is narrating in a way that only this particular individual in these particular circumstances could. Let's compare a passage from the opening of *Twilight* with an opening passage from *Parable of the Sower*:

> 'My mother drove me to the airport with the windows rolled down. It was seventy-five degrees in Phoenix, the sky a perfect, cloudless blue. I was wearing my favorite shirt — sleeveless, white eyelet lace; I was wearing it as a farewell gesture. My carry-on item was a parka.'
> — *Twilight*, Stephenie Meyer

> 'I had my recurring dream last night. I guess I should have expected it. It comes to me when I struggle—when I twist on my own personal hook and try to pretend that nothing unusual is happening. It comes to me when I try to be my father's daughter.'
> — *Parable of the Sower*, Octavia E Butler

The opening passage in *Twilight* tells us extraordinarily little about who Bella is. She is from Phoenix, her favourite shirt is sleeveless and made with white eyelet lace, and she carried a parka—a windproof jacket. It tells us nothing about what she wants, what she needs, her flaws, or her biases. It reads more like a weather forecast.

In contrast, *Parable of the Sowers* tells us that Lauren is conflicted: she wants to be the simple, carefree daughter of her father, but she is also reckless, knowing that there are terrible things going on in the world. It hints that she wants more. The particularity of the voice draws the reader in—we want to know more.

Delivering exposition in first person

Delivering exposition is hard enough but doing it in first person adds an extra layer of difficulty. It can be jarring if your character goes out of their way to describe something you would not expect them to—for instance mundane things like their day job, clothes, how their house looks, or physical description, leading to the cursed 'I looked at myself in the mirror' scene near the start of way too many young adult novels.

One good way to deal with this is the Difference Factor. In Suzanne Collins' *The Hunger Games*, the first chapter has the characters dressing up formally for the Reaping—a big event in their society where children are taken to compete in a deadly sport for television entertainment. Collins writes:

> 'Of course. Let's put your hair up, too,' she says. I let her towel-dry it and braid it up on my head. I can hardly recognize myself in the cracked mirror that leans against the wall.
> 'You look beautiful,' says Prim in a hushed voice.
> 'And nothing like myself,' I say.

This is a character describing themselves in a mirror, but it is not jarring because it does not give the reader information that the character would consider mundane or normal. It is focused on what is *different*: an elaborate and formal braid that Katniss would not usually wear. Describing something that stands out from the mundane also allows them to describe what the mundane usually is in contrast, a sneaky way to get in that ordinary exposition. What they would usually wear, where they would usually get their money, how they would usually look if that different thing was not happening.

Inference

You will also notice that this passage in *The Hunger Games* does not tell us that much explicitly about Katniss. It gives the reader a little about her hair, and that is it. Collins allows the reader to infer the rest. First-person writing uses inference a lot more than third-person writing because the author does not have the same ability to describe or tell you anything they want.

It would not make sense for Katniss to go on a spiel about how she looks, but just by being told that she looks 'nothing like herself' with a tied-up braid, a dress, and being very clean, the reader can infer what she might look like normally: rough hands from hard work, irregularly bathing because hot water is expensive, simple and comfortable clothes that can afford to get dirty. It becomes a very real physical description without ever going beyond what Katniss might naturally describe.

Inference can be used to describe places, objects, or anything else in the story that the narrator may not usually go into detail about.

> '… You describe the small things and let them imagine the large things. Which works very well. The small things are going to be very individual to what you're going to see that other people wouldn't, or things that everyone else would notice that your character glosses over.'
> — Brandon Sanderson[20]

The key is controlling what people will infer from your descriptions. What does your phrasing imply about the things around it? Consider this passage from *The Great Gatsby*:

> My own house was an eye-sore, but it was a small eye-sore, and it had been overlooked, so I had a view of the water, a partial view of my neighbor's lawn, and the consoling proximity of millionaires — all for eighty dollars a month.

Fitzgerald knew Nick Carraway, the narrator, would focus on how cheap it was, but he does not just describe his house as rundown with a thatch roof and broken cobblestone. Instead, he phrases it so we can infer how grand and beautiful the mansions

---

[20] Brandon Sanderson, Mary Robinette Kowal, Mary Anne Mohanraj, Wesley Chu "Description Through the Third Person Lens" (podcast, 12 February 2017) Writing Excuses <writingexcuses.com>

around it are. Rapunzel might only describe a single tower of a castle or James Bond only the smell of cigarettes, but how they describe those things will, by implication, give the reader a fuller picture of the world around them.

Sometimes, the reader can even imagine things better than you could ever describe them. This is the trick behind the 'unknowable horrors' of Lovecraftian entities. The unknown and imagined is nearly always scarier than seeing the thing in the flesh.

Confiding in the reader

A third-person story might describe the insecurities or secrets of a character, but a first-person narrator can uniquely choose to trust the reader with their secrets directly. Author of *Build Your Best Writing Life*, Kristen Kieffer wrote about the importance of crafting character voice:

> '[You can reveal] insights such as hopes, fears, prejudices, and regrets that your character might not be so quick to admit in their dialogue. In essence, your character's internal narrative builds a secondary dialogue that only your readers are meant to hear.'[21]

While this is true for character voice in third person as well, I feel it is particularly true in first person where the conscious decision to impart this information to the reader on behalf of the character is more meaningful. One of the opening lines in Giant Sparrow's 2017 game *What Remains of Edith Finch* is:

---

[21] Kristen Kieffer "How to define your character's unique voice" (21 February 2018) Well-storied < www.well-storied.com>

'My brother Milton disappeared when I was four. It was like the house just swallowed him up... The house was exactly like I remembered it. The way I'd been dreaming about it. As a child, the house made me uncomfortable in a way I couldn't put into words. Now, as a 17-year-old, I knew exactly what those words were. I was afraid of the house.'

Her first line is choosing to confide in the player about a family tragedy. The character is making herself vulnerable to the reader, and similarly to how you feel valued when someone confides in you, readers feel valued when a character opens up to them privately. The first-person perspective fosters this unique empathy.

Confessions make great opening lines and establish that uniquely personal relationship right at the beginning of your novel. The dual narrative—the public story and the internal secondary dialogue only for readers—is a real strength of the first-person perspective.

The first-person medium

Character voice is about how who the narrator is comes out in the way they tell the story. Medium refers to why and how they are writing it. Just like different characters will naturally focus on and exclude different things in their narration, the medium in which they are writing will shape how they tell their story.

The Last Time We Say Goodbye by Cynthia Hand eventually reveals that the book is written as a journal for part of the character's therapy following her brother's suicide. This is perhaps why the narration so purposefully confronts her difficult emotions and the ending is framed as her trying to find peace. What is described is not decided just by what happened but by *why* she is writing it.

Likewise, *What Remains of Edith Finch* is revealed to be a letter to the narrator's son—the last surviving member of the

Finch family. It is an attempt to explain his heritage to him, where he came from, which is why the story places such emphasis on generational trauma and the stories of distant relatives.

The Handmaid's Tale is revealed to be a series of audio recordings, which is why the narrative is loose, meandering, and conversational, often going on tangents. It reflects the way people talk.

Summary

1. A first-person perspective gives you the closest psychic distance, creating an engaging relationship between your character and reader, but you give up the ability to tell the story however you like. The reader's knowledge is limited by the character's. Deeply psychological stories thrive in first person.
2. Remove filter words that increase the psychic distance between reader and character. Use the implied 'I' to help your prose flow more smoothly.
3. Develop a strong character voice by asking what your character focuses on, misses, and which words, phrases, and metaphorical analogies they would characteristically use. This unique lens ensures the story is being told in a way only that character could.
4. Use the Difference Factor to get first-person narrators to describe mundane things. Consider what you want readers to infer from the limited descriptions your character might give.
5. Confiding in the reader can establish trust between character and reader and foster a unique kind of empathy. Consider how you can best use the dual narrative: the public versus the private internal dialogue.
6. Why someone is giving the first-person account and the medium in which they do it will also affect how it is presented and phrased, as well as its focus.

WRITING DARK LORDS

The Fellowship of the Ring by JRR Tolkien
The Wheel of Time by Robert Jordan
A Song of Ice and Fire by GRR Martin
Parting of the Ways written by Russell T Davies
Inkheart by Cornelia Funke
The Lion, the Witch, and the Wardrobe by CS Lewis
Avatar: The Last Airbender created by Mike DiMartino and Bryan Konietzko
Percy Jackson and the Last Olympian by Rick Riordan
Harry Potter and the Goblet of Fire by JK Rowling
Mistborn: The Final Empire by Brandon Sanderson

From Morgoth in Tolkien's *The Silmarillion* to Shaitan in *The Wheel of Time* to the Emperor in *Star Wars: Return of the Jedi*, dark lords have been a staple of the fantasy and science fiction genres since their conception. Mixed in with prophecies and paragons and hordes of minions, the dark lord is an irredeemable force for evil in the world. Sometimes their very essence is tied to the cosmic balance of good and evil, and other times they merely wield great power for the worse of the world. Exactly what defines a dark lord is hard to say, but we always know them when we see them.

We will be splitting this discussion into six parts: good versus evil, character arcs, dark lords are people too, creating an active villain, establishing the dark lord as a threat, and what to do when the reader becomes more attached to a secondary villain.

Good versus evil

Dark lords get a bad rap for being one dimensional. In the era of *A Song of Ice and Fire,* the rise of grimdark and *Malazan,* people have a soft spot for protagonists who murder children and burn people alive. There is a heavy emphasis on grey morality and deconstructing human moral binaries. Dark lords have thus become much a thing of the past, viewed as boring and simplistic because they do not play into this as easily. Most dark lords do not have the personal moral nuance we may be more accustomed to in our fantasy villains these days. However, I feel this misses the role dark lords can sometimes play in bringing thematic depth to the story.

Sauron is the Dark Lord of Middle Earth and is in fact the titular character of *The Lord of the Rings,* having created most of the rings we learn about, and especially the One Ring: 'The Lord of the Ring is not Frodo, but the master of the Dark Tower of Mordor' (*The Fellowship of the Ring,* JRR Tolkien). Sauron's role as the Dark Lord is not about deconstructing human morality, but about questioning the nature of evil itself.

The clearest example of this is in how the One Ring is destroyed. Gollum fights Frodo for it, and after biting off his finger, he takes it and dances over the edge, destroying the Ring and killing Sauron for good. Tolkien believed that evil is not undone by the great and powerful waging war, but by small acts of kindness. Tolkien emphasised mercy and pity:

'O Gandalf, best of friends, what am I to do? For now I am really afraid. What am I to do? What a pity that Bilbo did not stab that vile creature, when he had a chance!'

'Pity? It was Pity that stayed his hand. Pity, and Mercy: not to strike without need. And he has been well rewarded, Frodo. Be sure that he took so little hurt from the evil, and escaped in the end, because

he began his ownership of the Ring so. With Pity…
Many that live deserve death. And some that die
deserve life. Can you give it to them? Then do not
be too eager to deal out death in judgement. For
even the very wise cannot see all ends. I have not
much hope that Gollum can be cured before he dies,
but there is a chance of it. And he is bound up with
the fate of the Ring. My heart tells me that he has
some part to play yet, for good or ill, before the end;
and when that comes, the pity of Bilbo may rule the
fate of many—yours not least.'

Frodo and Bilbo both spared Gollum's life, and it is those
acts that allowed the Ring to be destroyed. This reflects Tolkien's
deeply held Catholic beliefs about the importance of mercy in
the realm of justice and virtue. After all, the Virgin Mary, a
crucial figure in the Catholic faith, is referred to as the Mother of
Mercy. Sauron as the Dark Lord being purely irredeemable
enables this discussion to focus on what it means to be virtuous
in the face of evil, to analyse the nature of evil—that it exists in
opposition to and overcome by mercy and pity.

On a deeper level, Tolkien is speaking to how evil will, in
time, destroy itself. That evil is self-destructive by nature. Sauron
is kept alive by the power of the One Ring—a power that meant
Isildur failed to destroy it in the years before *The Lord of the
Rings,* that Gollum kept the Ring for himself for hundreds of
years, and that even stopped Frodo from destroying the Ring
once he reached Mount Doom. The draw of power is irresistible
to mankind. Yet, in Tolkien's greatest display of irony, this is
also what gets the Ring destroyed, through Frodo and Gollum's
fight over the ring. The selfish drive to power will destroy itself
in the end, which really feeds into Tolkien's belief that 'evil', by
nature, is not a *creative* force in the world; that it cannot create
anything of its own, only *corrupt* that which has already been
made.

The moral complexity of *The Lord of the Rings* and Sauron's role as Dark Lord comes from the tension between the *cosmic* forces of good and evil, not human acts of good and evil. It assumes a fixed, inherent idea of evil, which can be a compelling starting point for a lot of people.

In Robert Jordan's *The Wheel of Time*, the Dark One takes on numerous forms across the series, but Jordan uses the Dark One to explore and contrast the difference between cosmic and human evil. Human evil is portrayed as petty, emotional, temperamental—almost childish—while cosmic evil is constant, permeating, corruptive, and controlled. Terms like 'cruelty' cannot apply to the Dark One in the way that they apply to Sauron because he is more a force of nature than a person acting upon the world. He is woven into the fabric of existence, a pillar of understanding how the world and free will works.

One character called the Betrayer of Hope is elevated by the Dark One once he moves past that childish evil and understands the importance of cosmic evil—its place in the universe. Jordan's story comments on how evil is not to be destroyed, but must be challenged, contained, and controlled.

Both Tolkien and Jordan use a dark lord archetype to communicate complex themes about the nature of evil that could not be accomplished as effectively if their villains were redeemable or partly good. This can get readers thinking just as much as Jaime Lannister pushing Bran Stark out a window sill, and perhaps even more. The nature of inherent evil, how we interact with it, whether it is a part of us, how we deal with it, and what it means to be good in the face of it are all interesting questions. Stories that deal with the subjectivity of human morality are almost incapable of looking at these questions because they do not assume an inherent good and evil, but rather that the moral fabric of the world is woven by our actions.

Where dark lords fall flat is when they lack this deeper meaning and purpose. When the dark lord becomes a one-dimensional obstacle whose defeat means little because they do not play an interesting role in their own right. If writing a pure evil dark lord, what are you saying about good and evil through their role in the narrative?

Character arcs

Some stories use pure evil characters to develop their heroes. In the BBC series *Doctor Who,* there is a species of purely evil creatures called the Daleks—they exist to 'exterminate' all other life in the universe and will not rest until they have accomplished this, believing themselves the only pure lifeform. During *Parting of the Ways,* our protagonist is put in a position to wipe them out for all time at the cost of killing billions of humans when the following exchange happens:

> EMPEROR: I want to see you become like me.
> Hail the Doctor, the Great Exterminator.
> DOCTOR: I'll do it!
> EMPEROR: Then prove yourself, Doctor. What are you, coward or killer?
> DOCTOR: Coward. Any day.

The Doctor here is forced into a corner: break his moral code or let pure evil win. Only pure evil pushes this arc to its highest point of tension because there is no negotiating with the Daleks, no ambiguity as to whether they will carry out their nefarious plan. The only way for the Doctor to stop them is to kill them here—at least it seems the only way.

A villain being pure evil does not mean your heroes are paragons. Pitting them against dark lords can test the limits of their morality: torture, murder, vengeance—whether these are inherently wrong or the ends justify the means. The Daleks here test how 'good' the Doctor truly is in a way no morally grey villain can. If you have a pure evil antagonist, then how does their evil heighten the tension in your characters' arcs rather than just being a thing to defeat?

The concept of a character foil is connected to this discussion: where a character's traits contrast with another character, usually the protagonist, highlighting the differences between them. Voldemort partly acts as a foil to Harry. Both were orphans who found their true home at Hogwarts, were magically gifted with connections to the founders, and brought into the fold by Dumbledore. But where Harry acts with love, Voldemort only pursues power. These similarities highlight the differences between the two of them. Namely, the power of love and friendship, a pervasive theme in the series.

Character foils are especially the case for fallen hero dark lords who once trod the same path the hero now walks. Their similarities will challenge the hero to ask who they are and where they are going, or in rare cases, it may make the dark lord question why they are doing the things they are. You have almost definitely seen dark lord figures dish out the 'we're not so different, you and I' line, which at this point is so cliché it makes the reader laugh. While this idea can be fun to play with, it only really hits home if the hero and dark lord genuinely share similar struggles and goals instead of vaguely similar backstories. Voldemort and Harry share near identical backstories but they do not share anything substantive that would cause Harry to think Voldemort may be right about enslaving humankind. The contrast is there for the reader to bring out the power of love and friendship.

Dark lords are people too

I think it is fair to say you can only endow a dark lord with complex characters motives so much before they are no longer a dark lord. Characters might be extremely cruel and narcissistic, presiding over an army of henchmen as Ramsey Bolton or Cersei Lannister do, but calling them a 'dark lord' fails to capture the context the archetype has built itself around. Even so, there is variation within the dark lord archetype that can remove it from the reader's expectations and make your character more interesting than they would otherwise be.

We have already discussed how Sauron from *The Lord of the Rings* and the Dark One from *The Wheel of Time* present different perspectives on evil and are thus different expressions of the dark lord archetype. Dark lords can have personality — viewing themselves as gods, as avengers for past wrongs, as a necessary force in the world. They can have a defined method of doing things. Perhaps they believe all living things need to be purified in fire, so insist on destroying their enemies with torches and pots of boiling oil. Alternatively, they may believe good is inefficient while evil is perfectly efficient, meaning they place a large emphasis on technological advances that maximise pain and damage with the littlest effort. Cruelty may not be a part of their method because cruelty is inefficient.

Give your dark lord a new way of viewing themselves, their enemies, goals, or their methods.

Secondly, there is an endless number of things that have no moral dimension and dark lords are not precluded from engaging in. A desire for death and destruction does not mean the dark lord cannot play the violin or enjoy apple pie. The White Witch from CS Lewis' *The Lion, The Witch, and the Wardrobe* enjoys collecting statues and putting them on display — of people she turned to stone, yes, but statues, nonetheless. It is a kind of vanity and extravagance that not all dark lords have. She also enjoys ensnaring and manipulating for the sake of it. The Adderhead in Cornelia Funke's *Inkheart* series fell in love in the years before he ascended to dark lord status. He is obsessed with legacy, with the idea of someone continuing on his position after him. Your character might be a 'dark' lord, but their armies, décor, and armour do not need to be fifty shades of black.

All these things give a more interesting character to the dark lord. The truth is readers like following *interesting* characters, and while a lot of writers have taken 'interesting' to mean 'morally complicated', these are not necessarily the same thing. Interesting can mean they look unique, speak in interesting ways, or they have a unique way of doing things, or do interesting things we have not seen as much before. This is not about making them relatable.

For a practical example, I love dark Scandinavian serial killer noir, and not because the serial killers are morally nuanced or complicated people, but because the killers are creative in all the worst ways. They are interesting to read about psychologically, even if they are about as close to pure evil as you can get.

<u>Creating an active villain</u>

Dark lords are notoriously absent in the story, preferring to send their henchmen and minions out to do the dirty work until the climactic showdown. As a general rule, villains who drive where the story goes, forcing the protagonists to react, who interfere across the story, feel more like a threat and seem more competent. The story remains tense because the heroes are put on the back foot. When the dark lord is the threat the heroes directly confront throughout the story, it makes the conflict more personal, intimate, and eventual losses and triumphs over them are more meaningful.

This is the reason the viewer is more immersed in the Zuko versus Azula conflict in *Avatar: The Last Airbender* than they are Aang versus Ozai. Zuko and Azula have both been around since the beginning of the series, continually presenting themselves as a major obstacle to overcome and being responsible for many of their greatest setbacks: Azula lightning-strikes Aang in the Avatar state, Zuko betrays Katara after she opens up to him, and Azula has a long-standing rivalry with Zuko. Ozai only appears three seasons in and never actually faces the heroes himself until the last moment. The only character with any personal tension with Ozai is Zuko, his son who he abused, but Zuko does not face Ozai in the finale. Aang does. As a result, there is a lot more catharsis in seeing Azula defeated than Ozai.

One thing that may help is to look at the high points of tension and emotional release in your story, especially those where the heroes lose. Ask whether the dark lord can be there in person instead of their henchmen or minions, letting that moment build into the protagonist's personal conflict with the dark lord rather than another character who may be less important.

<u>Establishing the dark lord as a threat</u>

There are two common reasons you might not use the dark lord as the antagonist the heroes repeatedly face. Some authors have recognised that it can be helpful to also have a more human villain on hand: Darth Vader in *Star Wars*, the Forsaken in *The Wheel of Time*, Luke Castellan in *Percy Jackson and the Olympians*. All of these have some level of humanity in them, redeeming qualities and more understandable motivations that complicate the narrative in a way that a 'pure' dark lord cannot. This allows for a variety of character interactions, arcs, and scenes between the protagonists and antagonists that you may not otherwise have available.

The question for you as the writer is whether you truly use that opportunity. Simply having another, lesser villain acting as surrogate for the dark lord needlessly splits the narrative attention between them. It can make both characters less compelling, especially if the surrogate is eventually cast aside for the heroes to face the Big Bad Evil Guy and the reader is expected to get all their catharsis from defeating the dark lord, when more of their emotions are wrapped up in the surrogate.

An incredibly common trope here is the henchman turning on the dark lord. Sometimes because they feel unappreciated, à la Shego in *Kim Possible*, or because they have a change in heart à la Darth Vader in *Star Wars: Return of the Jedi*. Both can be more compelling than the heroes simply facing a dark lord. This kind of plot twist often comes from the surrogate villain's redeemable traits winning through, their relationship with the dark lord souring, or some culmination of underlying tension that the reader has been following.

The second reason authors hold off on the dark lord themselves descending into the fray is to build anticipation. Antagonists are best established as a threat by showing the heroes losing to them, hurting the heroes in a way no-one else can, and demonstrating they are strong where the heroes are not. Consistently losing to the heroes book after book really undermines this. It shows the dark lord to be ineffectual and weak, so it can be helpful to hold them back for a bit when the heroes win.

With this said, an off-screen presence still has an impact in the story, like the monster in the dark before you meet them in a horror film. Stephen King once said that horror is all in the moment before you open the door and not whatever is behind it, and much is the same with dark lords. Throughout the *Harry Potter* books, a lot of emphasis is put on not saying Voldemort's name, insisting on calling him 'You Know Who' and 'He Who Must Not Be Named'. Characters liken him to a ghost that might appear if one recognises they exist, a demon that will crawl out of the mirror if you blink three times. Foreshadowing their return or arrival can deliver a powerful effect in the story and build up the character's potency. If they cast a shadow far larger than themselves, striking fear into the hearts of people even when they are not around, what will happen when they finally appear? The key is to deliver on this promise. When Voldemort finally appears in *Harry Potter and the Goblet of Fire*, four books in, Harry stands almost no chance against him.

This is because one way to build up the dark lord as a threat is to put the emphasis on the heroes hiding and escaping rather than defeating them. Harry has no chance to defeat Voldemort in the fourth book, and only survives by miraculously escaping using the portkey. This preserves the threat they pose the protagonist and makes eventually overcoming them more of a victory. It shows growth.

<u>Reader attachment to the secondary villain</u>

If the heroes repeatedly come up against the secondary villain rather than the dark lord, it is common for them to become more invested in that conflict than in the one with the dark lord, as noted in our section on creating an active villain. The secondary villain's defeat can be more cathartic, and this presents a structural problem: the third act climax may be less impactful because the highest point of tension turns on a conflict the reader cares less about.

Rick Riordan solved this problem in *Percy Jackson and the Last Olympian*. Luke Castellan is the primary antagonist throughout the series, the one the heroes face through most of the books, who is directly responsible for their greatest losses, even though the Titan Kronos is behind him. However, Riordan structured Castellan's arc so that the dark lord's defeat takes place structurally at the same time as Luke's and the dark lord's defeat comes out of the resolution of Luke's arc. Luke's desire to be a hero and his love for Annabeth are what ultimately lead to Kronos' downfall, and Kronos manifests himself *through* Luke Castellan. The battle with one is the battle with the other, keeping Luke the primary antagonistic force of the series with Kronos just giving his role extra weight.

Sanderson takes a different approach in *Mistborn: The Final Empire* by using mystery. The Lord Ruler is presented as a dark lord figure who does not enter the fray until the very end of the book. The heroes instead face inquisitors and other henchmen. However, Sanderson's story does not derive its catharsis from resolving a personal conflict between the heroes and villains so much as unveiling a mystery: the dark lord, the prophecy, the chosen one are all subverted. Where other authors use those structural changes to make facing the dark lord more interesting, Sanderson draws narrative intrigue from subverting our expectations of what it will mean to face the dark lord and who the dark lord is. It gives the reader a different kind of catharsis.

Summary

1. Writing a dark lord does not mean your story needs to be morally simple. Use their role to say something about the nature of good and evil.

2. Having a dark lord in your story does not mean your protagonists need to be purely good. Consider how coming up against pure evil might intensify your protagonists' arcs, and whether they can be used as character foils to underpin themes and define your characters.

3. Consider how you can be more creative with your dark lords by finding a different expression for their evil or giving them character traits outside their evil that make them interesting.

4. Active villains are present in the story. Allowing the dark lord to confront and harm the protagonists can intensify and personalise their relationship with the protagonists, making their eventual defeat more cathartic.

5. Having a more human secondary villain on hand can allow you to explore a wider variety of story threads. It can also allow you to build anticipation for the dark lord when they appear. Anticipation can also come from an emphasis on escaping rather than defeating.

6. If the reader is more attached to the heroes' conflict with the secondary villain, consider how you might structure the climax, making their defeat concurrent or fundamental to the defeat of the dark lord.

ON WORLDBUILDING

FANTASY AND ALIEN RACES

Story of Your Life by Ted Chiang
Dune by Frank Herbert
Axiom's End by Lindsay Ellis
Icerigger by Alan Dean Foster
Speaker for the Dead by Orson Scott Card
The Elder Scrolls series developed by Bethesda Studios
Stargate: Atlantis created by Brad Wright and Robert C
Cooper
Consider Phlebas by Iain Banks
The Belgariad by David Eddings
The Dragon Prince created by Aaron Ehasz and Justin
Richmond
Nightfall by Isaac Asimov
The Three Body Problem by Cixin Liu
West of January by Dave Duncan
Blade Runner directed by Ridley Scott
District 9 directed by Neill Blomkamp
Bright directed by David Ayer
Attack on Titan by Hajime Isayama

When fantasy and science fiction writers use the term
'race', they usually mean species: elves, dwarves, humans,
demihumans, dragonfolk, merfolk, treefolk, bluefolk, Louis
Vuitton folk. Given their prolific role in the genres, it is worth
discussing the factors you might consider when designing and
writing them. This chapter will be split into seven parts: realism,
where to start, biological pressures, culture, the Planet of Hats,
universal pressures, and the dangers of allegory.

<u>Realism</u>

Worldbuilders often put a lot of emphasis on realism—the logical consistency of the background detail supporting the imagined world—even to the point of treating it as a virtue, and while it is an asset to any world that strives for it, it is not the only or even most important element of worldbuilding. JRR Tolkien is often cited as being incredibly realistic. Elvish evolved with six different languages branching off from a proto-language, each with numerous regional dialects, varying pronunciation, and variations in alphabetical script, all of which sprung from the migration of different groups across Middle Earth; essentially, the way in which Tolkien's Elvish evolved within his imagined world carefully reflected the way in which languages evolve in the real world.

Yet at the same time, much of Tolkien's worldbuilding is not founded in realism. Dwarves somehow survive on a diet of meat while living underground, not cultivating any farmland. Hobbits somehow *only* exist in the Shire and cannot be found anywhere else in Middle Earth, despite living there for thousands of years. The difference in height between elves, dwarves, and humans did not evolve from any environmental pressures, and the only reason elves are better at *everything* is that Eru and the Valar made them that way. Tolkien balances realism and fantastical elements, and this is what makes his worldbuilding work.

Realism is important because it helps the reader buy into the less realistic parts of your story—a bit like slipping a pill you need into your food. Realism is not the end goal—immersion is. In *Story of Your Life* by Ted Chiang, there is an alien species called the heptapods who experience time differently to humans largely because of how their language works. As the protagonist learns their language, they begin to see time differently too.

This is based on the Sapir-Whorf Hypothesis which theorised that language can alter how one experiences the world on a chemical and experiential level. Scientifically, this theory is controversial at best, but *Story of Your Life* grounds this inside an otherwise realistic discussion of linguistics and biology. The line between fact and fiction is so blurred that by the end of the story, the reader totally buys Chiang's more far-fetched ideas because they are seamlessly woven together with the realistic ones.

Striving for perfect realism is not only impossible, but it can actively harm what you are trying to create. Immersion in stories is just as much about a reader being fascinated and wanting to know more. Frank Herbert's *Dune* features gigantic sand worms, but the realism of Herbert's desert and geology (which he spent years studying) is only half the equation. The other half is the sheer ungodly awe of these creatures. Their size, how they can devour whole buildings in an instant, the smallness you feel in the face of them — in other words, their effect in the story. Readers are not questioning just how a creature like that survives with the square-cube law. If Herbert spent pages and pages justifying the existence of sand worms to us, how they circumvent the square-cube law that prevents land animals reaching such a size, it would ironically get the reader thinking about problems with their realism they probably never have otherwise considered. It could even rob them of some of the majesty, terror, and awe they inspire. Not to mention, Herbert's narrative would likely grind to a halt under the weight of all that detail. Incessantly trying to assure the reader that a story element is 'realistic' can sometimes have the effect that the reader simply does not care anymore.

Internal consistency tends to be more important than strict realism when it comes to immersion with a fictional species, as it is with most worldbuilding. Realism can help readers buy the more fantastical parts of their design, but the how is not as important when the story treats those fantastical parts consistently. In *Story of Your Life,* how language affects the heptapods and humans is totally consistent across the story — we get an understanding of the underlying logic — the consequence being the reader does not get caught up in how realistic Chiang's creation might truly be. Chiang blends his technical explanations of both unrealistic linguistics and realistic linguistics such that it becomes difficult to tell which is which. Realism and consistency work in unison towards immersion.

A lack of realism only becomes a problem when the reader cannot immerse themselves in the unrealistic parts of a world or story, more often because they are internally inconsistent or so farfetched that they become inconsistent with the realistic elements.

Realism is also an important part of immersion in hard worldbuilding, discussed later in this book and contrasted with soft worldbuilding. Soft worldbuilding relies less on realism and uses mystery, unknowns, and the reader's imagination to create an immersive story. Refer to that part for a further discussion.

<u>Where to start</u>

Some people might advise starting with realistic approaches to how a species might develop scientifically: environmental pressures, competition with other species, and evolutionary paths. The truth is not only do most people *not* start with these things, but I do not believe actually helps create an interesting species. It might help with some degree of realism, but I do not find myself thinking about the size of the planet, the gravity it would generate, and how close it is to the sun when reading about fictional creatures. Most people simply start with an idea: creatures that can turn themselves into gases, beings born with their brain in their hands, tiny insects who build towers out of their dead. Tolkien began with the elvish language. Chiang began with a theme of free will and determinism in creating the heptapods.

My advice is this: take the kernel of your idea and discover its implications for your species from there.

Originality is hard nowadays. In 1907, Mark Twain remarked that:

'There is no such thing as a new idea… [ideas] are
the same old pieces of colored glass that have been
in use through all the ages.'

He was right in one way. It seems like we have an infinite
supply of elves these days. Wood elves, blood elves, night elves,
sea elves, space elves, kitchen sink elves. How many times have
you seen the honourable warrior race, the super advanced-
energy blade race, the bug-like hivemind species led by queens,
the short steampunk techno geniuses who live underground, or
the super advanced precursor civilisation that died in some
ancient cataclysm?

However, sharing the framing of these archetypes with
some author who came before does not mean you cannot do
something unique within that frame. Lindsay Ellis' *Axiom's End*
features a super-advanced reptilian species with mind powers
who live in a caste system—something we have seen before
several times. *Starcraft's* Protoss, Iain Banks' *Culture* series, the
Eldar in *Warhammer 40K*—but Ellis uses that template to discuss
the role genetics plays in defining who you are, just how
different aliens may be to humanity, and 'otherness' as a
concept. She tells an original story by picking up those pieces of
coloured glass and putting them together into a new picture.

Biological pressures

While it is true that a species can be anything you want it
to be, it is also worth recognising that certain features will arise
in certain cultural and physical environments. Biological features
and cultural practices do not exist in a vacuum and allowing
either your species to be informed by the environment or the
environment to be informed by the species can make the world
feel more interconnected.

Eating, reproducing, and surviving. These are the
shoulders upon which evolution stands. Consider the plucky
human in its natural habitat. As plants became scarcer in their

environment, humans developed the ability to eat meat, changing the shape of their teeth, how their organs worked, and their mating rituals. To hunt and defend themselves more easily, they developed weapons and tools from readily available stone and wood, but this would not have been possible without first becoming bipedal, freeing up their arms. In Alan Dean Foster's novel *Icerigger*, the alien tran developed claws like ice skates. They naturally developed them as they were advantageous in their frozen environment to help them escape predators and chase prey: eating and surviving. Larger claws then became a sign of a stronger mate, as it indicated hunting success.

The pequeninos from Orson Scott Card's *Speaker for the Dead* are a fascinating example of evolutionary science fiction. Their world was once ravaged by a disaster called the Descolada, destroying most life left on the planet. As a result, the only animals and plants that survived, like the pequeninos, were those that developed symbiotic relationships with one another that helped each other reproduce. The line between animal and plant became blurred. The Descolada also meant that the pequeninos had almost no predators, meaning they were largely incapable of defending themselves when humans came along and were not naturally aggressive towards them. They let humans watch and record them without fear. In both cases, the intimate connection between the species and their environment—with clear understandings of how their biology helps them eat, reproduce, and survive there—make the world come alive.

If you wish to justify or inform your fictional species with realism in this way, consider these questions:

- What type of food grows in their climate and environment, and how do they access it?
- Who do they compete with, and what abilities would help them compete?
- Who are their predators, and what abilities would help them survive?

- Which aesthetic traits would be selected for in their environment?
- How do they mate, and how do individuals choose their mates?
- How do they survive intense weather?
- What natural obstacles do they face in their environment, and which features would help them adapt to overcome these obstacles?
- What made each of your fictional species the dominant group in their environment compared to others?

There are endless questions you could ask, but these are just a few to get you started.

Culture

Culture is everything, including but not limited to architecture, politics, religion, clothing, class systems, traditions, technological development, sports, philosophy, legal system, prejudices, local myths, gender roles, military structure, the role of crime, the role of media, art, education systems, tourism, healthcare, housing, perspectives on death, social rituals, social etiquette, primary industries, the economy, and much more. Unable to deal with each of these in detail, we are going to narrow in on two aspects of culture in worldbuilding: how biological pressures affect culture and the Planet of Hats.

As an example of how environment influences culture, natural resources and forces important to a way of life in an environment will often show up in local religion. The Khajiit of Elsweyr in *The Elder Scrolls* series revere the moons Masser and Secunda because they dictate their birth cycles. They also use moon sugar in religious experiences.

However, it is a common mistake of simplistic worldbuilding to determine everything about a society according to the biological and environmental pressures around them. One of the reasons the wraith in *Stargate: Atlantis* seem hollow is that they have no cultural traditions or societal practices outside those associated with their survival instinct to feed vampirically off other lifeforms. They are a space-faring civilisation of people who are clearly individuals, but there is no sense that their class structure, artforms, or philosophies have changed over the millions of years they have existed, nor that they have any cultural appendages that are not dependent on their biological nature. This is akin to all human civilisation being dictated by our biological instinct to form groups and communities. These kinds of species feel static and unrealistic. The world lends itself to complexity before it lends itself to clarity. Gothic architecture did not develop in response to humanity's need to breed. Democracy did not purely develop to ensure our survival. It was the gradual systemic decentralisation of power motivated by social movements alongside the decentralisation of wealth.

As humanity has developed culturally and economically, we have become less subject to the dictates of our environment. Socially constructed pressures can override natural selection, especially when we can control our environment the way we now can. Consider developing cultural aspects disconnected from your species' biology. In Iain Banks' *Consider Phlebas*, the ethics of criminal punishment change drastically once a post-scarcity society is established, and massive orbitals change how the economy works as people can freely acquire land. The cyberpunk genre regularly touts how humanity has become independent of its biological bases.

The Planet of Hats

All dwarves are Scottish miners! All elves are poncy assholes! All orcs are honourable warriors who wield axes! The Planet of Hats is when an entire species, or even planet, is defined by a set few traits, and every character we meet from them fits them. In David Eddings' *Belgariad* series, the Chereks are all stoic seafaring warriors with axes and braided beards who sail longboats.[22] In other words, all members of society wear the same hat.

This is not necessarily bad worldbuilding, but it is not as nuanced or interesting as it could be. Eddings' *Belgariad* series is intended for a younger audience, but more mature readers are likely to be hungry for something more sophisticated. The reality is large societies are diverse economically, socially, politically, and morally. Species that reflect that deeper complexity are more interesting and immersive, but this complexity needs to be expressed through individual characters the reader meets. Which things would your species be divided on, both in the big issues and the small ones? Humanity has its own fair share of squabbling over all kinds of things.

Diversity of thought can create a more interesting culture. Phrases like 'the elves believe [x]' can be reductionist. What possible thing could you say all humans believe in? Perhaps only the sanctity of life, but even then, what life means is debated, there are some people who would disagree with that idea entirely, and how that belief finds expression can vary radically from society to society. Allowing the reader to see a lineage and cultural evolution in a species' beliefs, practices, and ideologies, as expressed through a diverse array of characters within the species, will make them feel less static.

Cultural identity is still a thing. Groups of individuals will share traits, histories, and interests that unite them and give them a sense of cohesion. This is also what gives rise to stereotypes. We imagine Spartans as fearless warriors because their cultural identity was so connected to war, but that does not make the stereotype accurate. Cultures have stereotypes, but individuals do not usually fit the stereotype entirely. In *The Dragon Prince*, the Moonshadow Elves are said to be fantastic assassins, masters of illusion, wise and fearless, and they live by a strong code of honour. Raylan is a Moonshadow Elf assassin,

---

[22] Hint: they're Vikings.

but she is full of fear and anxiety. Lujanne is a master of illusion, but she is not wise or knowing like Rayla expected her to be. Giving characters flaws or differences that undermine those expectations can be a great way to give the reader a strong first impression.

The Planet of Hats often manifests in a sibling: the Single-Biome Planet. Think *Star Wars'* forest world Kashyyyk for the wookies or *Dune*'s Arrakis, the desert home of the Fremen. The logic here is that because everything is one biome, all the planets' inhabitants take on some sort of character that reflects this. Realistically speaking, single-biome planets are out there, but once again, culture is more complex than the most basic of environmental forces, and a species will spread geographically if they can.

Universal pressures

In Isaac Asimov's 1941 story *Nightfall*, the inhabitants of Kalgash go mad, suffer brain damage, or even die after just a short period in nightly darkness because their world is surrounded by six suns and has had perpetual sunlight. Cixin Liu's *The Three Body Problem* takes this even further. An alien planet is thrown, almost randomly, around by the gravity of three different suns. This creates radical eras of scorching heat and intense cold. As a result, the aliens there evolved to dehydrate themselves during hot periods and hibernate during cool periods.

The science behind planetary forces like this is fascinating, complex, and infinitely varied. The only advice I can give is for you to study it closely if you want it to play a part in creating your fictional species. There is also a lot of room to create a unique species from universal pressures like this. Fantasy writers often rely reflexively on Earthlike conditions, but the universe offers an infinitely deep well to plumb.

Dave Duncan's *West of January* shows how universal pressures can affect culture on a planet that takes centuries to rotate. Half the planet is constantly freezing to death, and though civilisation develops, it is necessarily nomadic, constantly migrating every few decades to stay in the temperate zone.

The dangers of allegory

Fantasy and science fiction have long been used to explore social issues at a distance, with aliens and fantasy races standing in for groups in our society, either exposing the flaws of that group or making their concerns more palatable. This can be done well, and it can be done badly. The replicants in Ridley Scott's 1981 *Blade Runner* film are stand-ins for those broadly ostracized by society. The alien 'prawns' in Neill Blomkamp's *District 9* are stand-ins for Zimbabwean refugees coming to South Africa and are used to explore the country's history of xenophobia and racial apartheid.

This usually involves a degree of racial coding where a species is designed with traits recognisable as a particular group in the real world even if not explicitly intended to be and comment on that group. In a clumsy example of this, the 2017 David Ayer film *Bright* has orcs playing rap music, basketball, and wearing baggy t-shirts to tell the audience that the orcs are meant to represent African Americans.

Slapping a cultural label on a species that came from an entirely different biological and social environment to the one you are referencing can be jarring and may not the best way to key the reader into the real-world issues you are discussing. After all, one of the strengths of using science fiction and fantasy is the distance from reality that these genres offer. Personally, I find using a fictional species as a stand-in most effective when they face similar but not identical issues to those they are meant to be representing. Parallels can be drawn philosophically. Culturally and physically, the 'prawns' in *District 9* have nothing in common with the Zimbabwean refugees Blomkamp is discussing, but the xenophobia expressed by the characters and the violence, isolation, and dehumanisation they face mimics their real-world experiences. When this is done well, it gives you as a writer the chance to connect with a wider audience than a more direct story might succeed in reaching. Anti-refugee communities may have refused to engage with *District 9* if the film was more heavy-handed in its thematic delivery, but its subtle approach made it a hit with the general public.

A particularly difficult example to explore is Hajime Isayama's *Attack on Titan* series. There, a species called the Eldians are clearly paralleled to Jewish people. They are forced to wear stars on their clothes, to live in ghettos, and are killed with impunity by a Nazi Germany-esque power. On one hand, the story treats these people sympathetically. It shows them as victims of prejudice and xenophobia. On the other hand, characters justify oppressing the Eldians because they once controlled the world and oppressed others in turn. They can also be turned into monsters called 'titans' that eat people.

The problem with paralleling the Jewish people and Eldians is obvious: where does the allegory end? Is Isayama saying that Jews once controlled the world and *deserved* their persecution in the twentieth century? This would play into old racist tropes. The idea of Jewish people eating children is an old lie. Is Isayama saying Jewish people are secretly monsters on the inside? Whether these particular parallels were intended or not, a racist implication is present, and it is extremely uncomfortable. An inattentive reader, assuming Isayama did not intend this, may walk away from the story with that reading.

Drawing on racial imagery and issues from our world in fiction can be fantastic, but it can also lead to some terrible thematic conclusions if the author only draws on the *imagery* of a people group while ignoring the consequences of their depiction. If you wish to draw on the complex racial issues of our world, be prepared that people will interpret the whole story in that light, not just the bit you want them to. It may communicate things you do not intend.

<u>Summary</u>

1. It is more important for worldbuilding to be internally consistent than realistic. Realism frames the unrealistic parts, and the reader does not need to understand everything. Wonder and horror can be more immersive.
2. Start with whatever you care about: setting, culture, language, theme, or otherwise. Work outwards to build a logical world from there. Keep in mind these things arise from environmental, cultural, and universal pressures.
3. How does a species' physiology help them eat, reproduce, and survive in their environment? Consider giving them a unique reason to be the dominant species—superior resource collection or adapting more efficiently.
4. Biological pressures do affect culture, but they are not the end of culture. Developed species slowly override natural selection, especially if able to modify their environment. Allowing the reader to see how their culture has changed and diversified through a wide array of characters will make your invented species more nuanced.
5. Fantasy and alien species are sometimes used to explore modern social issues by coding the species to represent a particular group in society. Consider having the species face similar issues as a parallel rather than drawing on aesthetic similarities. When using allegory, drawing on imagery from real-world issues can risk people drawing thematic conclusions you did not intend.

WORLD HISTORIES

The Lord of the Rings by JRR Tolkien
The Handmaid's Tale by Margaret Atwood
Bright directed by David Ayer
Altered Carbon by Richard Morgan
A Song of Ice and Fire by GRR Martin
The Iliad by Homer
Remember Me created by DONTNOD
Harry Potter and the Half Blood Prince by JK Rowling

History is complicated. It is full of half-truths, legends, and way too many stories about Zeus having affairs as various animals. It is also a common part of worldbuilding. Fleshing out a fictional world is not just about understanding what the world *is*, but what the world *has been* in the past. In this chapter, we will work on developing a realistic, multi-dimensional world history.

Where to start

Around 1914, JRR Tolkien began working on the family of Elvish languages he is known for today. His passion for linguistics went so far for him to say that:

> '[My work is] fundamentally linguistic in inspiration… The invention of languages is the foundation. The 'stories' were made rather to provide a world for the languages than the reverse.'

Tolkien started his worldbuilding with the elvish languages. Given elvish splits into dialects, Tolkien knew that elves would need to divide geographically across Middle Earth over its history, allowing these dialects to evolve. Tolkien wanted the Avarin dialect to be the most distinct, indicating this was one of the oldest groups of elves to split off, and so he created a story that explained why the Avari split off so early: the Valar came to the elves and asked them to come to Valinor — a kind of heavenly land — and a small group of elves refused and stayed behind.

This is not me saying you should start with creating a language. Tolkien made something he loved an anchor and devised a world history that would explain how that thing came to be: why some dialects are more similar or different in vocabulary, syntax, and grammar. Building outward from elements you care about ensures a cohesive world that is realistically grounded, but it also keeps what you want to be at the heart of the reader's experience in the foundations of your world. You are not forced to somehow fit them in later.

This is, however, more of a worldbuilder's approach. Writers like Tolkien are interested in their world first and story second, and I think most writers are storytellers first and worldbuilders second. I know that I am, as well as other authors like Lois Lowry and Octavia Butler. Perhaps it may better serve you to extrapolate your world and its history out of things necessary for the story you want to tell.

In Margaret Atwood's *The Handmaid's Tale,* a story about a fallen America that gives rise to the oppressive and patriarchal Republic of Gilead, the story explores the female experience in a society where women are reduced to caregivers, mothers, and birthing vessels. Atwood wanted to explore the suffering of women worldwide:

> 'When I wrote *The Handmaid's Tale,* nothing went into it that had not happened in real life somewhere at sometime. The reason I made that rule is that I

didn't want anybody saying you certainly have an
evil imagination, you made up all these things. I
didn't make them up.'
— Margaret Atwood

To justify the story of this dystopia, Atwood looked to the
real-world causes of such suffering. Looking at Iran, Nazi
Germany, and the wave of legislation restricting women's rights
in the American south, Atwood set her story against an epidemic
of widespread infertility. She also knew Gilead needed to rise
out of a revolution or civil war. She understood that the kinds of
changes she was writing about are not usually the result of
incremental democratic change, but cultural upheaval, religious
fundamentalism, civil war, and revolutionary movements—all of
which have swept countries before and ended in women's rights
being diminished. While the exact events may not have
happened, history has played out similarly enough for Atwood's
story to be totally believable. Where Tolkien created a world
history that made sense of his languages, Atwood made a world
history that made sense of her themes and plot.

Constructing historical events to justify the story helps the
worldbuilding support the narrative, though the reader may
notice you are prioritising it over the world. The reader may also
notice if you construct a story out of the world you have created.
Whichever method you use, consider the natural causes and
consequences of storytelling elements you wish to prioritise. The
more your worldbuilding can frame and support the things you
care about, the better the reader's experience with those things
will be.

The problem with the Great Event

One thing to be aware of when creating a world history is
that focusing too much one a single event can lead to one-
dimensional worldbuilding. This is especially common in
fantasy and science fiction written by or aimed at younger
readers, where a great war or tragedy shaped *everything* about

the world: who hates who, who rules the kingdom, cultural celebrations and more.

The 2017 Netflix film *Bright* features a world much like our own but populated by more than one hominid species, with humans, elves, and orcs. Elves are rich, fashionable, magical, and beautiful, while orcs are thuggish, lower-class, and looked down on. The humans are about as human as you can get. The Great Event in *Bright* was a massive battle against the Dark Lord two thousand years ago. The orcs were mostly fighting for the Dark Lord while the humans and elves fought to stop him. As a result, the orcs are now treated as an underclass while the humans and elves reap the benefits of their victory an incredible two-thousand years later.

Two thousand years is a long time. In that timespan, humanity has seen the fall of the Roman Empire, the rise of the Mongol Empire, the slave trade, the birth and death of Brad Pitt in full denim. Even if there had been a devastating war some two thousand years ago, so much time has passed that its ramifications would be so abstracted from the present that it would be difficult to draw direct causal lines between then and now culturally, economically, or politically. *Bright*'s world feels stagnant because it extrapolates too much from that one Great Event. It would appear as if nothing else has changed *except* what was immediately affected by that battle. Despite two thousand years of history, that battle seems to be the only thing this fictional world history is impacted by.

A close comparison from the real world would be the life of Jesus Christ, whose impact can still be felt two thousand years after he was born. Christianity has had a profound impact on many societies across the globe; it has heavily influenced legal systems, art, morality, our traditions and celebrations, and how we dress and speak. Even so, the ways in which Christianity have shaped the world are infinitely more complicated than simply being a matter of Jesus' influence. Very little can be directly attributed to him, and more to the culture that has grown around and even independently of him. And, while a major influence in some parts of the world, he barely registers in others. While Jesus has had an impact on many societies, there are equally a thousand and more things he has not impacted that shape the world we know just as much or even more. Ice ages and wars and empires and plagues.

Understanding history means understanding that there is no single history. No single thing or event dominoed everything that has happened since, and following a single historical chain of cause and consequence to create your world will therefore feel one-dimensional. History is much more like a series of chains which link, unlink, get tangled, and then untangle themselves.

Great Event theory also applies to technology. At times, the world of Richard Morgan's 2002 cyberpunk novel *Altered Carbon* can feel dominated by the 'sleeve' technology that allows people to place their minds in new bodies, avoiding death. When discussing its political systems, its economy, its culture and religions, there is a distinct sense that Morgan's world is much the same as our world today except for how this re-sleeving technology affects it. For example, that the Envoys—special military units trained to regularly resleeve—cannot hold elected office. When writing science fiction, be careful to not rely too heavily on a single technology in examining how your world has changed.

This is also a criticism that can be leveled against Tolkien's *The Lord of the Rings*. For example, a Great Event that started a grudge thousands of years prior dictates much of the way elves and dwarves relate to one another to the point of deciding how Gimli and Legolas relate at the start of the story.[23]

---

[23] There is an exception worth noting here. 'Realism' is not necessarily the end goal for a writer (see the chapter on *Hard versus Soft Worldbuilding*). Some stories are written to be mythological grand narratives. Space operas, melodrama, and fiction aimed at younger audiences often do this. In these, Great Events and Great People and Great Technologies *do* dictate the world—intentionally and for effect—and that is totally okay. The difference is when it is not intended, or

The Pillars of History

You can look at history from many angles: politics, culture, technology, economics, geography, religion, war, trade, anthropology, sociology, and elsewise. Viewing your world through each of these lenses will tell a different story every time. If looking at the United States through the lens of politics, you might tell a story about democracy, human rights, how people were deprived of them, and how people fought for them. If viewed through war, you would tell a story of rebellion, civil war, becoming a world military power, and the complicated history of interference in other countries. If viewed through economics, then it is a story of slave labour, industrial power, and leading the world in free trade. What stories does your world tell through each of these lenses?

The perspectives of different nations or cultures on the same period of time will also yield different stories. The European 'Dark' Ages[24] were a golden age of academia and technology for the Muslim courts of Damascus. The period in which the United States became a world power was a time of decline for Britain. In GRR Martin's *A Song of Ice of Fire* series, the two continents of Westeros and Essos have wholly distinct understandings of world history. Westeros sees the Age of Heroes as a time of magic and great men and women, but Essos sees it as a time of terror with the Ghiscari Empire built on the backs of slaves. Even the Great Event which shaped the world — the Long Night — means different things when examined through different lenses. To a religious eye, it signifies the rise of the Lord of Light's religion. To a military eye, it was a hard-fought battle in the darkness by the living against the dead. To

---

when it seems like an oversight. *Attack on Titan* would be one such example, and arguably Tolkien's writing would be too. Both stories are unashamedly mythological at times.

[24] Which were not as dark as people like to think.

an anthropological eye, it saw huge swathes of people moving across the continent to find warmer places to live.

Consider looking at your world's history through each of these lenses. Imagine them as different timelines, seeing how they interact and affect each other. The more levels you do this on, varying from continent to continent or kingdom to kingdom, the more multidimensional your world will feel. A revolution will have economic and cultural consequences. The birth of a major religion will have economic and political consequences. World War I sprang from (among other things) a bunch of politicians advocating for war, the cultural glorification of war across Europe, and the fast-outcompeting German industrial sector. Caesar's assassination was a result of the Senate losing democratic power, the culture of deification of Caesar, and the dispossessed poor looking for alternative government after the economic failures of the ruling class.

Atwood does not rely on a single cause to create the Republic of Gilead in *The Handmaid's Tale* and *The Testaments*. Though we get very little information about the world beforehand, we know there were sociological causes with a demographic collapse following an infertility epidemic, religious causes with the rise of an ultra-conversative social movement, and political causes with an ineffectual Congress failing to address the needs of the populace.

The reliability of history and its records

It is one thing to know what happened historically and another to see what people *think* happened. What people believe and what parts of history survive and become formalised can be the result of bias, suppression, missing records, mistakes, and otherwise. Homer's *Iliad* details the history of the Trojan War, but it was passed down orally for a long time before being written down in the eighth century BC. While there is some historical evidence of a conflict during the Bronze Age, the details have clearly been embellished over the years, and we do not know how much information was lost.

Oral history can be mistranslated, with details omitted or added, and it relies on a chain of learning and remembering with a lot of room for fault along the way. Written records can be preserved for longer, and while this is no guarantee of their quality or truth, it does help preserve what the *original* message was. This is why the discovery of the Dead Sea Scrolls in the mid-1900s was so profound. It helped show how little had been changed in our records of the Old Testament. There is less room for fault or change in written texts, but that is not to say there is none. Written records can be rewritten, retranslated, or even edited as time goes on.

Primary sources are sources that witnessed the original historical event or that were at least produced at or very close to the time of the event. This does not make them infallible. Human memory is notoriously prone to alteration and can easily be convinced that something happened when it did not. But it does give a subjective insight into events at the time. How your history is remembered may change if there is a species on your world that lives for thousands of years. They may be more capable of ensuring the truth of the past is recorded correctly.

Technology has impacted the way we collect, store, and reproduce our records of the past. The internet today means more and more every day is recorded for posterity. We can consume more information about the past as well as our present than we ever could before because the world is more visible than ever. Ironically, the internet has given rise to a huge amount of misinformation as well. The truth is almost obscured by the huge numbers of lies.

DONTNOD's 2013 game *Remember Me* features technology capable of altering or wiping memories which is used to manipulate people into believing they suffered tragedies, had relationships, or saw certain things happen when they did not. J.K Rowling's *Harry Potter* series has a magical object called a Pensieve where people can store their memories, but in *Harry Potter and the Half Blood Prince*, we see that these memories can be falsified. Each of these offer fascinating worldbuilding implications for trusting historical records. You can use these to great effect—misleading characters and the reader into holding a false impression of history. This is a hallmark of Brandon Sanderson's writing; that the history as it is commonly understood is incorrect and the true history was obscured, twisted, or lost.

Who records the history is just as important as the way they record it. Did you know that Kim Jong-il was born atop a mountain, his birth heralded by a swallow, and when he arrived a star illuminated the sky, winter changed to spring, and a double rainbow arced across the sky? According to Our Glorious Leader, that is what happened.

People, nations, and organisations have biases; ideas that they want to promote or suppress for personal interest. The Saxon records of the 793 Viking raid of Lindisfarne describe the Vikings as, '[coming with] fiery dragons flying… heathen men made lamentable havoc' and later likening them to demons. Given they did not speak their language, wore what the Saxons considered inappropriate clothing, worshipped pagan gods, and the Saxons only experienced violence at their hands, it is no surprise that the Saxons would frame the Vikings so negatively.

Different cultures in your world, or even different people, will have different understandings and interpretations of historical events depending on how those events affected them. Is a conqueror a 'Great' or a 'Terrible' to them? Was a war a glorious adventure or a national tragedy?

How historical records change

Records get more abstracted from the original account the more time passes since it happened. Slowly, falsities, myths, lies, and misunderstandings creep into our understanding of even well-documented events. Despite World War II happening only eighty years ago, the belief that France failed to anticipate Nazi Germany marching around the Maginot Line persists to this day. The truth is we know that the Maginot Line worked exactly the way it was intended: to force Germany through Belgium and give France more time. That is almost exactly what happened. It was the strategic plan *outside* the Maginot Line that failed.

However, historical abstraction does not just happen because of bias and flaws in recording methods over time. Humans are intrinsically interested in explaining why things happened more than just recording the facts. This is why great ecological disasters were often turned into the mythological intervention of gods—not only do we like to give answers without having all the facts, but the simplest explanations are the ones easiest to pass on.

Historical narratives and personal identity

History links closely with our personal identity, how we view ourselves, our country, and how we relate to others around us. Our politics influences how we interpret our history. A white person and a black person may have a radically different relationship with the revolutionary period in the United States. To one, it is a fight for freedom, and for the other, it is the fight for the independence of a slave state.

This tends to intensify with recent events which enter our political sphere. Despite the Colonial Period having an arguably greater impact on how we live today, the Cold War seems to shape more of our political and economic ways of thinking. Part of this is because many people alive today, especially voters and those in power, lived through the fall of the Soviet Union, the war in Viet Nam, or even the Cuban Missile Crisis. They identify more closely with those events and their experience of them and vote accordingly.

This is partly why I find ancient grudges—such as those often depicted between elves and dwarves—to be shallow worldbuilding. I find it hard to believe that events so long ago continue to permeate the cultural consciousness in such a personal way, especially if those continuing enmities are based on a single event rather than a pattern of ongoing conflict that has lasted centuries. Great Events *might* heavily influence the scaffolding of our society, but it is uncommon for people to relate to an ancient event in a personal way.

One exception to this is religions, which are often built around personally connecting with events and people beyond your lifetime. Religions preserve the importance of certain historical events and attempt to establish a strong lineage between the past and present.

A second exception would be generational trauma, which sees historical events passing their *personal* impact down through generations. The legacy of the institution of slavery and the legacy of the Holocaust are intimately felt by the descendants of survivors. A Jewish friend of mine once explained:

> 'Unlike many Gentile children who might have the luxury of growing up without the concept of genocide, I literally can't tell you how old I was when I learned about the Holocaust. Sometimes it feels like I was born with this knowledge.'

These events stripped whole communities of their cultural identity, destroyed family bonds, and irrevocably changed the people they impacted. The consequences of historical events are preserved in a deeply personal and profound way—even if the individual was not there to experience them. It feeds into a sense of lost personal history and lost or changed community that individuals may more closely identify with or be affected by than even some events in their own life. It is worth considering how generational trauma plays into the relationships people have with history and the present—the stories they tell each other and the way they interpret the world.

Perhaps the most important type of historical narrative though is the national narrative. Rome's early history began with a war against the Sabines to the north which was likely a border dispute between tribes. But Rome always had a national historical narrative that their prosperity and triumph was divinely ordained. Thus, the 'records' of Rome's founding by Romulus—a son of the war god Mars—detail that this war against the Sabines was won by the intervention of Jupiter, king of the gods. The records of the Sabine War are not just altered by time and mistake, but by a national narrative that Romans told each other.

The United States has a national narrative of being the 'first real democracy', throwing off the chains of Empire, and leading the world as the freest country on the planet. The truth of this narrative is dubious, but it is undeniably powerful—both as a political tool and as a unifying cultural rally point. It changes how people vote inside the country and how outsiders view it. Many Americans have undeniably incorporated this narrative into their view of themselves, motivating them to do certain things—like join the military—and live certain ways.

In this sense, national narratives take on a similar role to religious experiences that draw a lineage between an individual and the past. Culture can create a sense of unity with people from the past; harms to them become harms to you and their triumphs become your triumphs. It is worth noting that this can be weaponised against people for the worse by creating an 'Us' and a 'Them' in the national narrative.

The question for you as a worldbuilder is this: what national narratives do your cultures have, and how do characters personally identify with that history?

Summary

1. Start with an element of your world or story that you care about and build outwards from there.
2. Great Event worldbuilding can feel hollow and stagnant, where the world is dictated overwhelmingly by a single moment, person, or thing. The world is more complicated than this.
3. Consider writing out a world history through different lenses: politics, religion, technology, geography, culture,

and economics. Then figure out causes and consequences for various events that interweave these timelines.

4. Historical records can be changed, falsified, embellished, or otherwise unreliable. Consider how this affects your world's recollection of its history, and the difference between what people say happened and what happened. Technology and magic can play into this in fascinating ways.

5. History is connected to personal and national identity. More immediate events have a greater impact on the political persuasions of individuals, except for religious experiences and generational trauma. Consider how national narratives may warp how history is told.

MONARCHIES

The Wheel of Time by Robert Jordan
A Song of Ice and Fire by GRR Martin
Avatar: The Last Airbender created by Mike DiMartino and Bryan Konietzko
Dragon Age: Inquisition developed by BioWare
The Way of Kings by Brandon Sanderson
Foundation by Isaac Asimov
Dune by Frank Herbert
Rebel's Creed by Daniel B Greene

Strange women lying in ponds and distributing swords is no basis for a system of government, but what if it was? We will split this discussion into seven parts: types of monarchy, constitutionalism, de jure versus de facto power, the three Cs, the royal court, how monarchies collapse, and why a good king a good kingdom maketh not.

Types of Monarchy

There are broadly two different types of monarchy that arise from different economic, political, and cultural environments: succession monarchies and elective monarchies. Succession monarchies pass power onto a relative or group of relatives of the previously presiding monarch. There are numerous ways this can happen, but you are most likely familiar with patrilineal primogeniture where the eldest son inherits all. An incomplete list of possibilities that have happened at various times in various places, some rarer than others, include:

1. Agnatic seniority → the monarch's younger brother inherits before the monarch's children.
2. Matrilineal primogeniture → the eldest daughter inherits before other children, even sons.
3. Ultimogeniture → the youngest son inherits before other children.
4. Proximity of blood → the heir is determined by the degree of genealogical kinship they share with the monarch.
5. Succession by trial → the heir is determined by who succeeds in a trial.
6. Partible inheritance → the inheritance is partitioned amongst heirs, though not necessarily equally.
7. Spousal inheritance → the spouse of the monarch inherits before the next in line.
8. Rota principalities → the brothers each inherit from eldest to youngest, to the fourth brother, before returning to the eldest son of the eldest brother who held the throne.

Across the thousands of monarchies over thousands of years in thousands of kingdoms, nation-states, and empires, there have been any number of slightly different variations on how succession works. But it is worth thinking about the circumstances that might give rise to one system over another.

Some areas of Japan practised ultimogeniture during the Edo Period. There was a cultural norm that valued caring for the elderly, and they recognised that the youngest child would be the one left doing this work while the older children had a greater chance to establish estates of their own. As such, the estate was left to the youngest child. The Mingangkabau society in West Sumatra, Indonesia, stands out as one of the few matrilineal societies in the world. Exactly how this happened is complicated and a bit of a mystery, with mostly cultural stories justifying it, but anthropologist Dr Peggy Reeves argued that it came from a special emphasis on *nurturing* and *growth* in their society:

> 'While we in the West glorify male dominance and competition, the Minangkabau glorify their mythical Queen Mother and cooperation.'[25]

Culture and religion inform how we construct and justify our power structures in society. Robert Jordan's *The Wheel of Time* is defined by its examination of gender and power. Only women are capable of wielding magic safely, and as a result, women occupy positions of power, wisdom, and influence in societies across the world. The Kingdom of Andor is only ever ruled by a woman, and the Amyrlin Seat—one of the most powerful positions in the world—is reserved for female magic-users. The magic system and unique dynamics of Jordan's world inform how the monarchies of this world work, as well as how people view the monarchy itself, not as a symbol of male predominance, but dependent on the wisdom of women. While our world has expressed prejudice against queens—viewing them as only a last resort in succession—this simply is not the case in Jordan's culture of succession. The gender dynamic also means that though the 'king' is powerful, they are not viewed as the ultimate power and wisdom in the world.

Elective monarchies can mean a number of things, but it involves some form of contractual consent between the monarch and their 'electors'. These electors can be members of the aristocracy, possible heirs to the throne themselves, or even in rare cases the people. The Vatican is probably the most famous example of this; the Pope has been formally voted in by cardinals since 1061 AD.

An elective monarchy does not mean that hereditary claims mean nothing. The Polish-Lithuanian Commonwealth was one of the most democratic states in history prior to the

---

[25] Christopher Ryan *Sex at Dawn: How We Mate, Why We Stray, and What it Means for Modern Relationships* (Harper Perennial, 2012 at 149-150

voting reforms of the twentieth century, on par with Ancient democratic Greece. It had an elected ruler, with kings' moots being called after the death of a monarch. However, despite any of the electors *theoretically* being allowed to take the throne, three monarchs came from the House of Vasa, each following their relative, while several other monarchs were at least distantly related. Blood relation became an advantage but no guarantee in many elective monarchies. Likewise, the magnates who exercised significant control over the poorer nobility could influence their vote during elections, meaning it was unlikely the lesser nobles would ever ascend to the throne.

Historically, truly elective monarchies have not often lasted long. Infighting, indeterminacy during the transfer of power, and ruling families using their position to concentrate power have all led to their collapse. Many successive monarchies began as elective monarchies until the ruling family accrued enough wealth and power to assert themselves. The Holy Roman Empire elected their rulers, but emperors nearly always came from the Hapsburg family, which held far more influence than the rest of the electors. The Hapsburgs became de facto hereditary monarchs of the HRE from 1438 to 1740. Over time, an elective body can become a 'rubber stamp'.

The bigger worldbuilding question is: what keeps your elective monarchy from devolving into a hereditary one? Sufficiently strong legal and constitutional protections, and a cultural emphasis on the right to contend the throne could support a system where blood relation is of little advantage. How does your kingdom prevent the ruling family or individual from positioning themselves to win the next election? In a modern liberal democracy, we protect the right of everyone to vote, criminalise suppressing the competition, and try to prevent people profiting off positions of power.

It is also worth considering *who* gets to elect and who gets to be elected. Elective monarchies, and even modern democracies, have requirements for who can do both things: age, sex, religion, ideology, experience, or elsewise. Your fictional culture will inform what your society demands of their monarch and electors. Fantasy has a history of expecting kings and queens to be honourable and have experience in war. It is easy to imagine an elective monarchy requiring military experience to stand. Alternatively, your church and state may be intimately connected, requiring a religious test before one can even vote. Perhaps a long-standing martial tradition means candidates must first prove themselves, *The Hunger Games*-style.

The Dalai Lama is the spiritual leader of Tibetan Buddhism—not quite a monarch, but a leader nonetheless—who is chosen from amongst children in a series of tests. These are heavily informed by Tibetan cultural beliefs around reincarnation, the nature of the soul, and the role of leaders in politics. Perhaps a similar practise could be found in your world, either for electors or candidates.

Whether a state uses a successive or elective monarchy is also connected to where conflict is likely to arise. Where numerous clans, families, or houses are constantly vying for power with no clear dominant party, elective monarchies are a measure to prevent territorial conflicts. Succession monarchies have been used to minimise conflict within a family or house by creating a clear, indisputable line of succession.

Constitutionalism

Constitutions create legal agreements, formal and informal, between the monarch and other bodies that limit the powers of the monarch. The degree to which the monarch is restrained will entirely depend on your society, and could range from the monarch possessing near-absolute powers to being merely a ceremonial figurehead. Constitutional monarchies as we know them today are often paired with rising living standards, an emerging merchant class, and a shrinking peasant class. Educated populations demand more of a say, leading to a constitutional agreement.

However, this is only constitutionalism in a modern context. Elective monarchies alone are a form of constitutionalism, restricting the power of the monarch to choose their own successor and informally demanding accountability by being voted in. Early examples of formal agreements like the Magna Carta in 1217 speak to a long history of groups ranging from peasants to the aristocracy demanding rights and privileges.

What are the social and political imperatives that constrain the monarch in your society? The 1688 Glorious English Revolution was partly motivated by Protestants seeking to restrain an ardently Catholic monarch, King James. This led to the constitutional right of '[Protestants to bear] arms for their defence suitable to their conditions' and preventing the establishment of ecclesiastical courts designed to punish people for not conforming to the monarch's religion.

Which powers matter in your society? When we think of constitutions, we think of rights in court, tax, and the right to vote. These are typically negative rights, but your constitution does not necessarily need to reflect this. Following the 1905 reforms in the Russian Empire, the constitution enshrined the right to form unions and protest. This right only took on constitutional importance because of the especially harsh economic conditions and political tensions with communists in the Russian state. It is not a right we see in many other constitutions, and your society will have powers and rights that arise from its specific cultural and historical context.

If your world features a special resource that the whole community depends on to survive during the winter, then rights to that resource might be enshrined in the constitution. An era of witch-hunting may result a right of passage for witches to travel freely. A plague may mean peasants demand the right to a decent burial. Do not assume the way constitutions work in our world will work for yours.

<u>De jure and de factor power</u>

Worldbuilding a monarchy is just as much about how power is *legally* divided (de jure) as it is how power is *factually* divided (de facto). We already discussed how all electors in an elective monarchy may *legally* have the same vote, but certain families will *factually* wield a lot more influence.

The Prince of Pentos in GRR Martin's *A Song of Ice and Fire* is legally the elected monarch, but the real power in the city lies in the hands of a small number of nobles called magisters—the city is actually ruled by an aristocracy, not a monarchy. We discussed before how some elective monarchies become 'rubber stamps' for a particular family, but this is the opposite dynamic. Sometimes electors wish to maintain the elective monarchy because they know they wield more power, as the magisters do, so long as it persists. A hereditary monarch might diminish them, so they do their best to thwart any attempts to get rid of the Prince.

The 1870 to 1947 Empire of Japan was an aristocratic oligarchy with power divided amongst several powerful families as well as the Emperor. It saw a similar dynamic to Prince of Pentos. The aristocrats beneath the Emperor preferred to keep the Emperor in power, even if they could theoretically have removed him, rather than allow a rival to take over, all because they knew a new monarch or democracy would diminish their role in government. The Earth Kingdom in *Avatar: The Last Airbender* is a bureaucracy where power truly lies in the hands of the state ministers despite it formally lying in the hands of the Earth King. Over decades, the ministries have slowly eroded the de facto power of the monarch under the guise of them being a 'cultural figure' who should not dirty their hands with politics.

In all these cases, elective and hereditary, powerful vested interests play a game of diminishing the de facto power of the monarch without risking their own. What matters is that the dynamic between ruler, ruled, elector, and elected are never as simple as we might imagine, and it is worth pinning down just how these dynamics work in your society.

Creating a combination or balance between a couple of systems of government by dividing de facto and de jure powers between different groups can give your world an extra layer of complexity. The Roman Empire is sometimes imagined as an absolute monarchy of sorts, but it was truly more of a stratocracy with military leaders holding significant sway over who ascended to the throne and which laws were passed and enforced. Who is your monarchy biased towards and against? Who does the monarch have to fear? Who does the monarchy need to account for first?

These questions will be closely linked to the social structure and economic systems of your society. In BioWare's 2014 game *Dragon Age: Inquisition*, the Archon may be the usually hereditary monarchical figure of the Tevinter Imperium, but the wider society is a strict racial class system with elves being viewed as racially inferior. There is also a magical hierarchy above that governing who wields power, wealth, and commands status in society. It is also a slave-based economy. While the Archon may be the legal head, most of the workforce, resources, and wealth is controlled by other powerful human mages. The result is a magocratic-monarchy where mages hold sway over the city, and even over the monarch.

A communist social or political structure will have strong ties to unions or working-class representatives. A capitalist economy may mean corporations or CEOs hold greater sway over the monarchy and society than your average person. A monarchy may be at the heart of society, but how is the society's workforce, wealth, resources, and social capital organised? These will each inform where power truly lies.

Even in the most absolute of monarchies and governments, rulers are still beholden to those who keep them in power: the military, the church, ministers, or others. The Mad King Aerys II in *A Song of Ice and Fire* was legally a near-absolute monarch, but his rule depended on Tywin Lannister, who managed the money, workforce, resources, propaganda, and nobles in such a way to keep him in power. When Tywin decided to switch sides, that was the end of him. It is also worth noting that at a certain point Tywin recognised that circumstances had changed to the extent that he could gain more by opposing the monarchy than by supporting it, which is a constant question monarchs must grapple with. If they do not, they collapse.

Even without a constitution, monarchies will always be restricted by the desires, motivations, conventions, and culture of those who keep them in power.

Communication, control, and commerce

We discussed these three factors in the chapters on empires in the first volume of *On Writing and Worldbuilding*, but they operate on monarchies in a few specific ways that are worth covering.

Communication is how quickly information can be relayed between the central authority and its provinces. The quicker and more detailed it is, the easier it is for a monarch to exercise personal control over their dominion. The challenges of a pre-modern setting are obvious. Historically, some monarchs developed itinerant royal courts that moved throughout the country. Emperor Henry VI of the Holy Roman Empire travelled more than four thousand kilometres in 1193 across his dominion to reassert loyalties and reaffirm control. Communication becomes less of a problem when the ruler can place themselves wherever they need to be most.

Ögedei Khan, the second khagan-emperor of the Mongol Empire, put a lot of resources into developing the Örtöö network in in early 1200s: a system of checkpoints with horses and shelter that allowed messengers to easily travel twenty or thirty miles per day across the vast kingdom. Not only did this greatly improve the efficiency of the Mongolian army, but it facilitated trade across the empire and reinforced the power of the emperor.

In Brandon Sanderson's *The Way of Kings*, this communication barrier is overcome with magic in the use of spanreeds—a comparatively fast way of transmitting large amounts of information across great distances akin to a telegraph. The lords and ladies can spend all their time at the warfront while maintaining a great degree of personal control over their distant domains.

Isaac Asimov's *Foundation* series is set during the collapse of the twenty-five-million planet strong Galactic Empire. The story makes a point of the fact that the outer regions are becoming independent. Even if their treaties recognise the Emperor's legal authority, there are no meaningful obligations to the Crown, nor or any consequences should they not fulfil them. In other words, they are independent in all but name. Asimov also points to how communication with the capital planet Trantor is extremely slow, which makes it incredibly difficult for the Emperor to enforce his will on the edge of the galaxy. These things all contribute to the collapse of the Empire.

One can work out the degree of control a central authority might plausibly exert by asking why the people would remain a part of the state, especially when the state comprises a collection of disparate cultures and ethnicities who each wish to preserve their identities. Itinerant courts helped with this. The Early Egyptian Dynastic Court held the Following of Horus where they travelled about the country to not only be more visible to subjects, but to exert influence directly over the diverse cultures in the outer regions, as opposed to through viceroys. The fear of direct intervention was always maintained.

Monarchs also used systems of patronage to ensure loyalty. Rewards and punishments were used to keep the aristocratic class dependent on the Crown for money, power, resources, position, and influence. In our world, these commonly included titles, land, economic rights, and government positions. The Qing Dynasty granted the right to wear peacock feathers, a complex and important symbol in Chinese mythology and religion, to those who served the Emperor well. Queen Elizabeth I was known for her cunning use of the patronage system to set the nobility against one another, never letting one become powerful or influential enough to challenge her, while also providing enough boons to ensure their loyalty. In an age where power came from your land, she rewarded subjects with the loan of important lands but retained their ownership herself to maintain the power of the Crown. In contrast, in *Foundation*, the Emperor granted whole planets and powers to the aristocracy beneath him in perpetuity, rather than by loan.

Consider what elements might be used in your system of patronage. Perhaps particular resources are especially valuable in your world, and rights to them prized. Perhaps there is a species of especially intelligent, hard-working, or powerful people that the Crown owns and loans out to nobles who impress them. It could even be that the monarch themselves is the literal source of magic, and their patronage involves divvying up that power amongst the loyalists.

The galactic empire in Frank Herbert's *Dune* series maintains power through a system of patronage. Similar to *Foundation*, the Emperor gives and takes away lands from those who please or displease him, as he did by giving House Atreides the planet of Arrakis just before the beginning of the first book, but there is one important difference. In *Dune*, the Emperor controls access to certain spacefaring technologies and space travel. Where in *Foundation* the nobles were not kept in competition but made wholly sufficient with no need to serve the Empire, the nobles in *Dune* are made dependent on the monarch, akin to Elizabethan England. At the heart of any system of patronage is the question of what is valuable and what constitutes punishment in your society.

Monopoly grants—the right to be the sole profiter of a particular thing—are sometimes used for patronage. Elizabeth I temporarily improved the English economy by granting patent monopolies for new inventions, but monopolies soon became so unrestricted and common that:

'[There were] harmful consequences that became a serious grievance under the harsh economic

conditions of the 1590s [for] "by lycenses a fewe
were enriched and the multitude impoverished"'.[26]

However, it is important to note that myths have always
surrounded the notion of an 'absolute monarch'—at least in the
way most people commonly understand the term. Monarchs
would commonly promote people they trusted and demote
people they did not, delegating power to minimise the need to
communicate while maintaining a degree of control. The
worldbuilding questions for you are: who does the monarch
trust or not trust to maintain their power and which democratic
or constitutional norms or power structures make this strategy
more difficult, thus weakening the monarch?

Commerce is crucial in maintaining the stability of the
state, and it can be interesting to look at how the monarch
interacts with the economy. They can make it better or worse.
Fixed capital cities with the monarch's permanent residence
became more common as financial centres developed.
Constantine moved the capital from Rome to Constantinople not
only for security reasons, but because Rome was declining while
Constantinople controlled the riches of the Black Sea trade.

The Royal Court

Royal courts are not just what you see in *Game of Thrones*.
Arabic, Asiatic, European, and African royal courts each worked
differently with different praxis, positions, and power structures.

The Japanese Imperial Court has a tradition of *saibara*
songs which come from songs sung by those transporting tribute
to the Kyoto capital in the past, signifying the importance of this
procession. Europeans are accustomed to titles like Duke, Baron,
or Lord being hereditary, but in the Qing Dynasty, titles were
sometimes downgraded with each generation, placing emphasis
on how far removed you were by bloodline from the person who

---

[26] Rosemary Sgroi "Monopolies in Elizabethan Parliaments" The
History of Parliament <https://historyofparliamentonline.org/>

earned it. Traditions in royal court come from historical realities which may not exist in your world, so transplanting (for example) the 1577 French royal court into your book can feel unrealistic to the reader. While there is nothing wrong with finding inspiration in the real world, it can also be worth making your own traditions deeply rooted in the unique context of your story.

Factions within the royal court might be vying for power. While it is easy to imagine these as lords and ladies, history is full of different kinds of people playing court politics. Eunuchs were a powerful class in the Ottoman, Vietnamese, and particularly Chinese imperial courts. They would even interfere with the line of succession, appointing themselves as regent rulers and accruing significant wealth and power. The Praetorian Guard, a military body, held a lot of sway over who became Roman Emperor before Constantine abolished them. Likewise, exactly *how* these factions and individuals vie for power may change. In Daniel B Greene's *Rebel's Creed*, the noble classes of the Ruzzai people fought to control art collections that depicted their cultural stories. Owning certain pieces lent you respect and influence, akin to controlling important religious artefacts. Consider unique ways people might exercise power in your world.

Positions in our royal courts have historically put emphasis on land ownership, but this need not be the case in your world. In Robert Jordan's *The Wheel of Time* series, the Amyrlin Seat is a powerful female mage that most royal courts pay heed to, keeping a position for her advisors and whose authority is almost never questioned. This position intentionally reflects the importance of female magicians in this society and the power they wield.

How monarchies collapse

Eventually, all heads roll, especially if you are a French monarch. Monarchial governments can fall in much the same way and for many of the same reasons as any other kind of government, so this section will focus on where a monarchy may be different. It is easy to focus on how monarchy has declined in the face of the rise of democratic power, but monarchies have been overthrown across history whenever competing powers have found it advantageous.

Dozens of African monarchies were virtually wiped out during the Colonial Era by supposedly democratic powers for primarily economic gain. The Albanian monarchy was destroyed in 1939 and replaced by Mussolini, a fascist. Monarchical collapse is not necessarily democratic or good.

But monarchs, being elevated figures accustomed to wealth, worship, and symbolic importance, often did fight against growing constitutional and democratic norms. The surviving monarchs today—the Norwegian King, British Queen, Danish Queen , Swedish King, Japanese Emperor, Tongan King, Thai King, and many others—adjusted to new constitutional demands and divested their powers. Those that did not or did not do so quickly enough ended up lined up against the wall.

We discussed before how some cities can become financial centres, forcing the monarch to move to them. This kind of economic transformation can also lead to tension between the monarch and merchant classes as the monarch might resist a trade city becoming their centre of power. It may read as a symbolic acknowledgement that power truly lies in trade and the merchants who control it. As the financial classes grow, they may be less dependent on the monarch for influence or protection. You could use this mark the decline of a monarchy and the ascendancy of a mercantile regime.

No matter the period—ancient, modern, or in the future—there will be a tension between the monarch and other powerful groups within society. Consider who has which powers, which powers are contested, and where that relationship is heading. Is it getting worse, getting better, or on the brink of collapse? If your story is about the collapse of a monarchy, then this tension will likely be a long-term causal factor in how that comes about.

A good king a good kingdom maketh not

There is a famous quote from GRR Martin in discussing Tolkien's worldbuilding:

> '*Lord of the Rings* had a very medieval philosophy:
> that if the king was a good man, the land would
> prosper. We look at real history and it's not that
> simple. Tolkien can say that Aragorn became king
> and reigned for a hundred years, and he was wise
> and good. But Tolkien doesn't ask the question:
> What was Aragorn's tax policy? Did he maintain a
> standing army? What did he do in times of flood
> and famine? And what about all these orcs? By the
> end of the war, Sauron is gone but all of the orcs
> aren't gone – they're in the mountains. Did Aragorn
> pursue a policy of systematic genocide and kill
> them? Even the little baby orcs, in their little orc
> cradles?'[27]

If your kingdom is unstable, then it is almost never simply because of a bad monarch, and if your kingdom is prosperous, it is almost never simply because of a good monarch. Propaganda and the rose-tinted glasses of history shape our view of particular monarchs as good or bad, but these stories are always more complicated. It is not helped by the propaganda of the time aimed at making their leaders look good.

King Louis XVI of France was the monarch at the time of the French Revolution, but he attempted numerous reforms to make his realm more democratic and transparent. The problem was the culture of the nobility around him who were increasingly ostentatious and greedy. Those who were disenfranchised naturally had an axe to grind, and being a

---

[27] Interview with GRR Martin, Author of *A Song of Ice and Fire* (Rolling Stone, 23 April 2014) transcript provided by Mikal Gilmore

symbolic figurehead of the nobility, that axe, just as naturally, fell on Louis' neck. Monarchies exist at the heart of complex systems, and sometimes nobody, not even the king, can truly control them. Like how we discussed that no monarch is truly 'absolute', the culture that surrounds the monarch is often outside of their control. Placing all of the blame on the monarch can make your world feel simplistic when history never is. While Tsar Nicholas II was ineffective and ignorant in his time as monarch, the wheels of revolution had arguably been set in motion long before he ascended to the throne in 1896.

Rather than focusing on individual personalities, it can be more helpful to think of a monarchy's collapse in terms of the economy, the environment, and culture. Natural forces like drought, famine, good harvests, storms, long summers, and short winters are largely outside the monarch's control while being major factors in the stability of a state. The Zhao Dynasty adopted the Mandate of Heaven, which meant disasters were an indication of the Emperor losing the favour of the gods. Long periods of natural disaster sometimes led to their overthrow.

While monarchs can regulate the economy, they cannot control the interactions of thousands of individuals across their dominion. Downturns and upturns are often the result of complicated market forces, and yet the monarch can receive both praise and blame for these. Likewise, while the monarch influences culture, they cannot control the complex interactions between class, religion, and community—all of which can make a state stable or unstable.

Asimov recognised that these forces are more powerful than any given individual. He wanted the *Foundation* series to be about technology, economics, and religion as the movers of society. He rejected the Great Man theory, even going so far to not have consistent main characters in his book. The Galactic Empire is specified to have collapsed for a variety of complicated reasons rather than from the incompetence of the Emperor personally:

This enormous population was devoted almost entirely to the administrative necessities of Empire, and found themselves all too few for the complications of the task. (It is to be remembered that the impossibility of proper administration of the Galactic Empire under the uninspired leadership of the later Emperors was a considerable factor in the Fall.) Daily, fleets of ships in the tens of thousands brought the produce of twenty agricultural worlds to the dinner tables of Trantor…

Its dependence upon the outer worlds for food and, indeed, for all necessities of life, made Trantor increasingly vulnerable to conquest by siege. In the last millennium of the Empire, the monotonously numerous revolts made Emperor after Emperor conscious of this, and Imperial policy became little more than the protection of Trantor's delicate jugular vein…

While the monarch can be at fault or deserving of praise for some things, if you want to worldbuild your kingdom to be prosperous or poor, come up with economic, natural, and cultural reasons for this that are outside the monarch's control.

<u>Summary</u>

1. Monarchies are usually either elective or successive, through which type of succession will be heavily dependent on the specific story context of your world. Consider what things will change how succession works: who is preferred, who is eligible, and who gets which powers.
2. Consider where the de jure and the de facto power lies in your society by asking who controls the wealth, resources, people, and social capital. Absolute monarchies are never truly absolute and are always kept

in power by those around them. Figure out who these are, their interests, and the powers they have in turn.

3. Consider how communication, control, and commerce factors into how much power your monarch can exercise, how they exercise it, and how successful they are. Patronage is often used in a carrot-and-stick way to maintain power.

4. In worldbuilding a unique royal court, consider drawing from Asiatic, Arabic, African, or other less familiar models to set yours apart. Find unique traditions that arise from your unique story context, as well as unique court positions and titles that reflect your wider world and the factions vying for power.

5. Monarchies do not just collapse because the monarch was terrible, nor does the decline of their power necessarily come from democratic influence. Likewise, monarchies do not prosper and suffer merely because of a good or bad king. The culture, economy, and environment are each powerful forces outside the monarch's control but vital to the stability of the state.

PLACE NAMES

The Lord of the Rings by JRR Tolkien
A Song of Ice and Fire by GRR Martin

Have you ever thought about how we called the planet we live on 'Earth'? Dirt, the soil we stand on, basically. But it got that name because it is descriptive. It is what it is, and it is about all humanity can agree on. Coming up with place names is difficult. In this chapter, we will give an overview of how they start, how they change, their relationship to power structures and migration, and at the end we will go through a detailed, step-by-step example of creating a fictional place name together with everything we have learned.

How they start

Place names tend to have some mixture of three dimensions. They tell us something about the place, its history, or the people who live there. Dr Peter John Drummond, linguist and topologist, observed

> 'Place-names are born when language meets topography: overwhelmingly place-names refer to natural or man-made landscape features, the names persisting even if the features disappear… [though]

it would be more precise to say when 'culture engages with topography'.'[28]

Take the River Avon, for example. 'Avon' means river in Welsh. The full name means *river river*. Dozens of towns across Europe took on the suffix -chester, -caster, and -cester from the Old English adaptation of the Latin word for castle or fort: 'castrum' and 'castra'. Such forts and protective stones walls were built across the Roman Period, and cities took on names denoting these man-made features. The moral of the story here is that our ancestors were not that imaginative.

With this being the basis of most place names, do not feel like you need to create an entire language just for naming the places in your world. A lexicon of some basic terms may help: forest, river, hill, valley, farm, castle, village, or whatever other features dominate your world's landscape. These would give you a good basis for suffixes and prefixes. For example, in JRR Tolkien's *The Lord of the Rings*, 'Minas' means tower in Sindarin, which is why it often appears in compound names throughout Middle Earth. Minas Tirith means 'tower of the guard' and Annúminas 'western tower'. The words listed above all tell us something about the place itself, be it natural or man-made. Usually, a more important feature in the area; either what it is primarily used for, what is dangerous about it, what helps navigate it, or what dominates the landscape. In ancient times, these names were attempts to communicate something important about a place as clearly as possible in as little time as possible over distance.

Secondly, names from history. Gregory McNarmee described place names as a kind of 'fossil poetry':

'[Names] afford a kind of folk history, a snapshot in time that enables us to read in them a record of

---

[28] Dr Peter Drummond "An analysis of toponyms and toponymic patterns in eight parishes of the upper Kelvin basin" (M.A (Hons), M.Sc PhD thesis, University of Glasgow, 2014)

important events and reconstruct something of the culture of the namers at the time they assigned names to the places they saw.'[29]

The name 'Matanza' in the Florida Matanza River means 'slaughter', taking its name from a Spanish massacre of French Protestants that happened there in 1565. It was an important event in the region's history, especially considering the Protestant legacy of the United States. For a fictional example, King's Landing in GRR Martin's *A Song of Ice and Fire* is named for the place that King Aegon landed and built his first fortress before his conquest of the continent. It was a pivotal event in Westerosi history that brought the region into a new era. Even though a series of hills dominate the landscape, and it is the capital of the kingdom, it is no wonder that it takes its name from this historical event. In both cases, the historical narratives of cultures in the region contributed to the naming of each place.

However, these are less common than topographically determined names like the River Avon. Consider limiting names like this to more critical historical events; ones that enter the social consciousness of those not from the area. These names fall into usage because large numbers of people recognise the event and this recognition feeds into the cultural zeitgeist. The smaller and more local the landmark, the fewer the people it would need to take its name from an event. A local spring may be named for a town's founding, even if none of the other nearby towns register this.

Thirdly, a place name might tell us something about the people themselves. The topographical feature the name highlights or how they frame historical events that happened there can tell us about the culture of those who lived there. Boston was originally called Trimount by early European colonists—named for the three large peaks that dominated the

---

[29] Gregory McNarmee *Grand Canyon Place Names* (2nd ed., Bower House, United States 2004) at 7

landscape. Native Americans tribes called the same place Shawmutt, meaning a place of water to ferry across. The European name emphasises the land they were first able to colonise, while the Native American name emphasises the water around it as an important travel route for living in these lands. They tell us different things about the ways of life and what this area meant to these two different groups.

This is also often the case for places named after historical events; using terms like disaster, peace, victory, or tragedy characterise the event itself, rather than just describing what happened. They tell us about what that event means for the people coining the name. If the Spanish had remained the dominant power in Florida, then perhaps the Matanza River would have dropped the term 'slaughter' and picked up 'reclamation'. After all, the Protestants were wiped out after settling on supposedly Spanish-claimed land.

This is also why different nations or groups of people often use different names for the same place. The Sea of Japan is the stretch of open water between Japan and Korea, but Korea has long insisted it be called the East Sea, while North Korea labels it the Korean East Sea. Using a name with 'Japan' or 'Korea' in it suggests geopolitical ownership or hegemony in the region.

A fictional example of this would be Tolkien's Osgiliath, meaning 'City of the Stars'. The city was centred around a Great Dome that looked to the sky—an important geographical feature, yes, but more importantly, the name echoes back to how important stars were in Númenorean culture. Gondor holds itself out as the last bastion of Númenorean blood, and so this connotation is important to them.

Even so, when a name tells us about the people who live there, it is most commonly what they call themselves. England is the land of the Angles, Scotland is the land of the Scots, and Russia is the land of the Rus. There is nothing wrong with this simplicity. Simple names stick. Simple names make sense.

How names change

Names can change for several reasons. One is that the language itself may evolve. Perhaps the word 'lake' changes to 'lark' and Lake Michigan becomes Lark Michigan. The dominant language in the region may also change, with the new speakers adding modifiers to the original name for clarification. This is where you get wonderful tautological names like the River Avon which, as we noted before, means *river river*. The Normans did not understand Welsh when they took over in 1066, so they added their own word for river, 'rivere', just to make sure all the new people knew that the big blue thing was a river. Mount Maunganui in New Zealand means Mountain Big Mountain.

Names can also change when they become simplified. Modifying words like 'of', 'the', and 'on' are removed as people use it more and more. The remaining word is a husk of its previous self. New Zealand's largest lake was originally called 'Taupō-nui-a-Tia' until it was simplified to 'Taupo'. Translated, this changes the name of the lake from 'the great cloak of Tia' to simply the 'cloak'.

Simplification removes words, prefixes, suffixes, or syllables that are harder to pronounce, especially when a new dominant language moves into the region. For example, Tolkien's older elvish word for 'dreadful' was *gêrrha*, but this evolved over time to be *gaer*, losing the accent and a few letters to be simpler to say.

A third way a word might change is with conflation. Suffixes, prefixes, or even whole words or symbols may sound like one another, especially to foreign speakers who move into the region. Over time, similar-sounding words can be conflated, resulting in one being eliminated from use, or combined, resulting in a new word being formed. Remember how we discussed coming up with a simple lexicon for basic geographical features? Consider which sound similar, which are complicated to pronounce, and which could be conflated or simplified. For example, the word *frith,* meaning woodland, and the word *firth,* meaning watery inlet, have been conflated in historical maps. We no longer use the former.

Names can also change with elaboration, when people add modifiers, not because the language has changed or the name has lost its meaning, but to distinguish it from other places with the same name. You will have seen this with 'greater' and 'lesser' or 'big' and 'little', or with additional geographical descriptors if the land itself has changed. The Spanish named several places after flowers or trees that no longer grow there, and so additional descriptors have been added to elaborate on the places these names refer to.

In the course of this discussion, the prospect of new speakers moving into an area has come up numerous times. Whether refugees, migrants, invaders, or colonists, people moving into a region can radically change the language spoken there—both the one they encounter and the language they bring with them. Consider where borders have changes in your world historically, where disasters and war have created refugees, where empires have risen and colonised and then fallen. All of these will change how language and culture have meshed, giving rise to different place names.

A great example of this is the city of York. The Danes controlled a region in England called the Danelaw following the invasion of the Great Heathen Army. Danish words like 'howe' for 'village' and 'thorp' for 'hamlet' bled into the Anglo-Saxon style of names for the region. The city of York went from the Old English Eoforwic to the Old Norse Jorvik, eventually ending up in the Middle English York, combining elements of both languages. Even though the Danes were eventually pushed back, these linguistic traits have remained in towns and cities they lived in. Consider mapping out where ethnolinguistic groups have moved throughout your world historically and which language traits they would leave behind, even if a new dominant language or culture takes over afterwards.

Power

Naming a place can be a powerful act. Alexander the Great conquered Persia and named seventy cities after himself—and one after his horse. As funny as this is, it was an act of ownership, pride, and a show of power by the Macedonian king, erasing the name of his enemy and replacing it with his own.

The Greeks and Turks have a tumultuous history of war and tragedy, and many Greek nationalists refuse to recognise Istanbul by its current name. Instead, they call it Constantinople—a callback to the time when they conquered it. In their eyes, recognising the Turkish name would be conceding ownership. This power struggle over a name resulted in Turkey's refusal to deliver mail if the letter did not bear the name Istanbul.

The name of the Russian city of St. Petersburg was changed in Petrograd in 1914 because it sounded too German, and Germany was the enemy during World War I. Later, in 1924, it was renamed again to Leningrad as Lenin and the Bolsheviks came into power. Petrograd was originally named for Tsar Peter the Great, and after the overthrow of the Tsarist regime during the Russian Revolution, the Bolsheviks felt having a city named after a Tsar did not reflect their values. It did not reflect the power structure in what was now Soviet Russia.

These names are about exerting control, cultural and political, over a region, and the most common way this naming struggle is expressed is through endonyms and exonyms. Broadly speaking, endonyms are names bestowed on a place by those who live there while exonyms are names bestowed on a place by those outside of it. For example, Caledonia was an exonym given to what we now call Scotland by the Romans. The name came from a Roman description of the place or people as 'hard'. Scotland is more an endonym, a name given by the Gaels to their land. At the time, however, Caledonia was the more widely used name outside of Scotland because the Romans held power in the region.

For a fictional example, in Tolkien's *The Lord of the Rings.* The Entwood is a great forest in the south of Middle Earth, but it is an exonym used by humans to describe where the ents—giant tree-beings—live. The ents themselves use a different name that means *sunrise forest* because they remember when their forest extended to where the sun rises. This name is never recorded or remembered by anyone else because humans control the lands around them, as well as what information is passed on, and how the maps are designed. In each of these cases, which names fall into use is much more about who is in power, and not simply which might be the better-sounding name.

This is one of the reasons why colonialism has been such a powerful force in terms of how we think and speak about place. Indigenous populations will usually have their own endonym for an area, but these are commonly overridden by the name imposed by the colonisers. For example, the Maori name for my own post-colonial country is Aotearoa, meaning Land of the Long White Cloud, but colonial powers named it New Zealand after a region in the Netherlands, Zeeland. Given colonial power became dominant in the region, that is the name that stuck.

The fact that there are more places with Maori names in the North Island rather than the South Island reflects how ninety per-cent of the Maori population live there. Indigenous Maori names are far less common in the South Island where European culture is a lot more dominant. Consider which places have been colonised in your world, presently or historically, by who, and how that relationship has affected place names. This becomes even more crucial at important geopolitical sites that hold cultural, religious, or political value.

Names not only reflect power, but also politics. Following a government initiative to revitalise the Maori language over the last three decades, the name Aotearoa has become widely used and recognised in official documents, maps, and classrooms where it was not before. There has also been an active effort to put the Maori name on signs and maps around New Zealand to give it equal treatment, leading to the endonym and exonym holding more equal status in common parlance.

A practical example

Imagine a small village built around a waterfall that provides fresh water to its inhabitants. These inhabitants also believe that their god is made of water. Because of this, they name the place after the waterfall itself. They call it Divine Falls, or in their language, Mirthunfell.

Over time, the word 'Mirthun'—divine—is simplified to 'Mirth' as the 'un' is easy to leave out when you say it quickly. The name of the village is now Mirthfell.

Their land is then invaded by a foreign power and a new people move in to settle the region. These people have trouble pronouncing the 'th' blend. They also do not speak the language of Mirthfell and do not realise it means divine falls. To add clarification, they add on a word that means water in their language: polm. The result is that most people now call the village Polm Mirthfell. This name is recorded on maps and it falls into use as their people dominate the region politically and demographically. In time, the name is simplified even further with the 'fell' section and the 'th' sound being dropped.

The place is now called Polmir, even if it is officially recorded on maps as Polmirth.

<u>Summary</u>

1. Place names most often tell us something about a central geographical feature—manmade or natural—the people who live there, or an important historical event that happened there. What it highlights tells us something about the culture of those who named it: what they value, what they fear, what they emphasise. Consider creating a simple lexicon of natural features to draw from.

2. Names change across history as languages evolve, speakers simplify the name, segments of the name get conflated with other terms, or people add modifying words to help define the name for them.

3. Migration leading to languages mixing is important to consider. This often happens along tense borders and trade routes, via colonialism, or as refugees flee war and disasters. It can be interesting to see where ethnolinguistic groups have lived or travelled historically by their syntax, lexicon, or grammar being passed on through place names.

4. Which place names are recorded, survive, and are used can be an exercise of cultural power. Endonyms are names given by those who live in a place; exonyms are given by outsiders. This is particularly common in colonised regions.

CLASS, WEALTH, AND POWER

The Great Gatsby by F Scott Fitzgerald
The Culture series by Iain Banks
Starcraft developed by Blizzard
Shadow and Bone by Leigh Bardugo
The Witcher series by Adrezij Sapkowski
The Stormlight Archives by Brandon Sanderson
The Handmaid's Tale by Margaret Atwood
The Testaments by Margaret Atwood
The Wind Singer by William Nicholson

Class, wealth, power, and status are powerful forces in determining how people within a society interact. They are also immensely complicated; a few chapters in this book will not be able to address them in totality. As always, the best research is studying real-world examples for yourself. Over the next few chapters, we will discuss the nature of class and caste systems, how they are maintained, and how they change and fall. These are aimed at giving you enough of an understanding to serve you in worldbuilding these things, not to make you an expert. They will hopefully prompt questions for you as a worldbuilder, adding depth where perhaps there was not before.

Wealth, power, and status

Sociologist Max Weber described 'class' as the relationship between three things: wealth, power, and status. He called this the Three Component Theory of Stratification: groups of people can be divided along these lines within these three categories to be a higher or lower class.

Wealth, power, and status do correlate and even create one another — a person with wealth is more likely to have power and a person with power can use it to find wealth — but they are not dependent on each other. F Scott Fitzgerald's *The Great Gatsby* is all about how no matter how much money Gatsby acquires, he can never attain the same status as those born into 'old money' like Tom Buchanan. The book is a fascinating look at the complex interactions between these three things in 1920s American society. In William Nicholson's *The Wind Singer,* power comes from academic achievement in the novel's rigorously meritocratic society but being a member of the upper rings only guarantees a particular type of job and status, not wealth.

An upper class with all the power but none of the wealth or status and a lower class with all the wealth but none of the status are equally unlikely.

Wealth, power, and status correlate in different ways depending on cultural context. In *The Great Gatsby*, there is an undercurrent of moral, racial, and genetic supremacy to the concept of 'old money' while 'new money' is looked down on. At the time, the last holdovers of the Victorian aristocracy were dying out in America, and the relationship between status and wealth is a lingering remnant of that old order. How wealth, status, and power correlate today has changed as our cultural context has changed:

> 'Today's top executives are devoted work-
> worshippers… these individuals aren't working out
> of necessity… It's about the display of productivity
> as a symbol of class power. In an era of extreme
> inequality, elites need to demonstrate to themselves

and others they deserve to own orders of
magnitude more wealth than everyone else.'[30]

Where in the past status could be based on a belief that the
aristocratic class were inherently more worthy, society now
worships the work ethic, which in turn acts as a justification for
extreme wealth. Broadly speaking, inherited wealth does not
command the same status in our cultural context. Both then and
now, wealth and status correlate, but *how* they correlate has
changed. What does your society culturally value and how do
people exert political power? These will each help define the
bounds and requirements for wealth, status, and power in your
society.

Historically, class structures in human society have been
predominantly organised by wealth. Land was intimately tied to
the power you could exercise over others and the money you
could make, and status flowed from that. There are any number
of reasons this may not be the case in your fictional world. In
Iain Banks' *Culture* series, humanity has reached a post-scarcity
society known as the Culture. Not only is land no longer the
main avenue to wealth, but money itself has ceased to exist in
the way we think of it now. Everybody can live the life they wish
with society automated by artificial intelligences. As a result,
'class' is primarily defined by status—the parties you are
allowed to attend, the respect and social capital you command.
Wealth and power mean little in the Culture. The ultimate
punishment of the lowest class of criminals in no longer being
invited to parties.

Alternatively, a civilisation built around a hivemind would
have little use for status as a concept. Status is about the relations
and hierarchy between individuals, but a hivemind might
stratify themselves into 'classes' of workers, warriors, and
leaders without there being any real distinction in the status of

---

[30] Ben Tarnoff "The new status symbol: it's not what you spend—it's
how hard you work" *The Guardian* (United States, 24 April 2017)

each. Instead, they become necessary functions of the greater whole. While the Protoss in the *Starcraft* universe are not a hivemind, they are connected to each other in a vast psychic network. They are born into some roles more than others, and the line between status and purpose gets intentionally blurred. Power inherently lies in the hands of those with the greatest psychic abilities.

It is also worth noting that the de jure and de facto lines between each class may differ. During the Edo Period in Japan, peasants technically held a higher position in the cultural and religious hierarchy than merchants. The logic was that peasants created something of value for society while merchants simply profited off the labour of others. Yet the peasants had no wealth, power, or status of their own like merchants did. Merchants often owned estates and wore more lavish clothing, and they had more rights than the peasants in practise, who were not permitted to leave their lords' estates. It is worth considering whether there is a difference between the outwardly held beliefs about class and the reality in your society.

The more important point here is that when designing a class structure, a single pyramid of stratification will rarely fully encompass the complexities of wealth, power, and status. The economy, culture, and politics of society are always changing and a little out of sync with one another. The colonial era involved masses of wealth, power, and status being transferred to European populations, but even with the civil rights movements of the twentieth century, these things are still not equitably distributed. Technical equality does not match the reality. It takes time for changes in one to influence the other.

Social mobility

Social mobility is how you acquire or lose wealth, status, or power and move between the classes—up or down. The Song Dynasty in Ancient China is a rare historical example of an ancient community with relatively high social mobility. The lower classes could acquire power, status, and even eventually wealth through an imperial exam:

> 'The second basic concept [of Confucian philosophy] is that the feudal order... could not be salvaged unless it was based on the principle that the wise, able, and virtuous should rule... it insisted on giving men equal opportunities... the competitive civil-service examination system became a permanent... channel for the recruitment of members of the ruling class.'[31]

Though rare for low or middle-class people to get this opportunity, it still happened, and academic excellence became an avenue for social mobility. Families gained a foothold in government, and with that came status and wealth. In Leigh Bardugo's *Shadow and Bone* series, magical prowess becomes a quick way to acquire power. Magic-users, 'grisha', are given better pay, status, and privileges in the military that commonfolk do not have. They are also commonly resented as a result— viewed as upstarts and undeservedly privileged by the rich and poor alike. Perhaps your world values military prowess or the ability to resist a kind of magical plague that has infected the world. People able to fill these niche roles may be more socially mobile.

Studies have borne out that education is a vital factor in social mobility:

> 'Class differences [in the UK] are almost 100 times higher than race differences, as 24 times is 2,500 per

---

[31] Pang-Ti Ho "Aspects of Social Mobility in China, 1368-1911" (1959) 1 CSSH 330

cent. The class segregation involved in access to higher education is huge.'[32]

The technology of the Industrial Revolution may have created economic opportunities for a rising middle class by freeing up their time and allowing them to upskill, but it was the new education system that underpinned that. Widespread education worked against the class divide by diversifying their job opportunities. Where before the upper class learned French and polo while the working class learned how to sew and build, children from both were suddenly learning similar skills.

Educational opportunity closes the economic gap in a class system by narrowing the skill gap between each class. If you want a highly stratified class system, then one way to do this is to restrict the educational opportunities available to groups. If you want a class system that is slowly breaking down, then consider a widespread education system undermining those differences. This happened because of the Industrial Revolution in our world, but it may come more from an Enlightenment movement in yours or a religious movement. After all, the Reformation saw the Bible translated into the language of the layman.

Each of these things can make social mobility easier, but it is also worth considering which things make social mobility harder in your world. The Umayyad Empire required religious conversion if you were to acquire any seat of power, and they levied taxes on those that did not convert. The racial hierarchy espoused during the Colonial Period made it nearly impossible for indigenous groups to attain any wealth, status, or power. Andrzej Sapkowski's *Witcher* series is an interesting example of magic making you socially mobile but lowering your status. Witchers are viewed as outcasts, almost inhuman vigilantes who kill monsters, even if they are employed by lords and kings.

---

[32] Danny Dorling "Class Segregation" in *Considering Class: Theory, Culture, and the Media in the 21st Century* (Brill, United States, 2017) chapter 15.

There will be chosen and inherent attributes that make ascending the social hierarchy harder, and you could create an interesting tension between those who want to conserve the social order and those who do not.

Magic and technology

All of this is really about the incentives and barriers in your society, which are further complicated by magic and technology. Not everyone will necessarily face the same barriers or have the same incentives when they have drastically different capabilities. In the previous chapter, we discussed how certain attributes will make social mobility easier or harder, and technology and magic are two such things. When it comes to fantasy and science fiction, this intensifies.

The simplest example of this is that Superman does not need to worry about earning money like your ordinary working person. He gets sustenance from the sun. Fewer barriers may make Superman more socially mobile—able to attain wealth, status, and power. In contrast, if being in the 'upper class' means being cruel and capricious, then it will be harder for Superman to rise in the ranks. He is all about Truth, Justice, and the American Way after all. What does climbing the social ladder *incentivise* people to do, and what barriers might there be for some people that are not there for others?

Magic and technology can threaten the way these incentives and barriers work. The Industrial Revolution saw a huge shift in class structures with a rapidly expanding middle class as technology allowed smaller businesses to thrive. People were finding new ways to climb the social ladder, and with that, our ideas of status began to change. A similar thing may happen with magic, where a significant group no longer needs to rely on the wealthy and powerful to attain what they want.

Caste systems

Caste systems are slightly different to class systems, but also more similar than you might think. Caste systems stratify people along the lines of wealth, power, and status with the distinction of your caste being overtly determined by things you cannot control: where you were born—such as the Japanese Burakumin, or your family—like in the Indian caste system. Caste systems will sometimes have a class of 'untouchables'. The concept of caste attaches a moral weight to certain existences in a more explicit way than class systems. These influence the jobs you can have, where you are allowed to live, the positions of power you can attain, and the perception others have of you on a fundamental level.

In Brandon Sanderson's *The Stormlight Archives*, there is a caste system that divides people between those with light eyes and dark eyes. Culturally, those with light eyes are viewed as natural leaders, and they use this to justify their positions as kings and nobles. While it is possible to change the colour of one's eyes in *Stormlight* by acquiring a magical blade, this is incredibly rare. It affects how the characters interact with one another and view themselves. Caste systems make social mobility incredibly difficult.

Humans are not naturally born into roles. There are no meaningful distinctions between sexes, races, families, or cultures that demand stratifying society along rigid lines. But fiction complicates the idea of a caste system because this is not necessarily the case in a fictional context. An alien civilisation may very specifically give birth to workers, warriors, priests, and leaders in a way that humans do not. Stratifying their society may be an entirely natural thing.

Even so, class and caste systems are not as different as you might think. In a sense, there was a caste system explored in *The Great Gatsby*: Gatsby could not acquire a particular status because he was not born into 'old money'—something he could not change. Though the concept of an 'untouchable' is something we in the west largely associate with non-European social structures, gay people have long been treated as an untouchable underclass whose very existence is immoral. How differently are 'untouchables' treated from a young single mother who served time in prison for doing drugs? These people often end up socially isolated, excluded from jobs, looked down upon, or even ostracised from their communities—a kind of moral puritanism we mostly see in caste systems. Though not formally laid down in any social doctrine, the practical realities are much the same.

In 1984, scholar Dr Abraham Thomas compared the racially segregated United States to the Indian caste system:

> 'Once divested of its exotic names... the caste system is nothing more or less than any system of social inequality involving changing patterns of domination, exploitation, and rebellion... I would submit the traditional race relations between blacks and whites in the US are strikingly similar [wherein] state and national political structures in both countries are overwhelmingly controlled by the dominant group — the whites in the USA and the upper castes in India.'[33]

The key distinction, it seems, is that caste systems often have a religious or philosophical backbone to them to justify why people should be explicitly divided along these lines. This is often based in historical narratives or religious texts. Of course, even this is a hard line to draw. It was not so long ago that Divine Right, based on biblical theology, justified the rule of kings and queens.

Margaret Atwood's *The Handmaid's Tale* and *The Testaments* are a good case of that blurred line between a caste and class system. Gilead is a theocratic patriarchal society that very clearly divides men and women into two different classes. Men have nearly all the wealth, power, and status while women are stratified into marthas, aunts, handmaids, and wives. Their

---

[33] Dr. Abraham V Thomas "Is There a Caste System in India?" (1984) 2 Bridgewater Review Article 7

theology presents this stratification as natural, needed, and equal. The de jure belief is that men and women are two parts of the same whole playing different roles, but the de facto reality is that women are second class citizens.

There are also large swathes of the working population that make up a class system independent of this, and how they interact forms several interesting character interactions in the story. It is not nearly as simple as theology determining how people relate. A caste system is in play even if the society does not recognise it as that. If you have a caste system, then consider what the exact justification is for it, as well as how it may intersect with a class system independent of it.

Class culture

Classes have cultures within themselves: how they talk, what they wear, what they eat, what they do for fun. In our world, the wealthier wear expensive clothing and yell at each other over mahogany tables while the poor eat cake and wear cheap, mass-produced garments. Silk was a mark of the Imperial Family in China for a time as it was an especially rare and beautiful resource. A rare mineral may be a sign of class or status in your world. Polo is an expensive sport; a horseback game played by the upper class, but perhaps horses are so commonplace in your world that they instead bet on lizard fights.

The biggest factors at play here are accessibility and cost. What is readily available to each class, and what is rare or difficult to acquire? These will inform the major differences between classes. The growth of the middle class can be partly attributed to the expansion of free trade across the nineteenth and twentieth centuries. As goods and materials became cheaper and more widely available, the dividing lines between classes broke down. The status signifiers slowly lost their meaning and cost barriers lowered. A gemstone no longer required the same wealth it did before; it did not confer the same status. The culture of each class changed as their opportunities rapidly expanded. They became much less dependent on the upper class for any kind of wealth, especially as labour laws were introduced.

Even so, this is not the only reason for differences between classes. Perhaps the biggest misconception is that all classes or castes will share the same values, practises, and status symbols. They do not. While there will be significant overlap—after all, how else would they measure social mobility?—different classes are acted on by different pressures. These will in turn give rise to different traditions, values, religious sentiments, and practises.

Different political rights for Athenian women as a class led to the festival of Thesmophoria which became 'increasingly associated with the lower classes by the last quarter of the fifth century'.[34] A religious divide developed as the Roman poor adopted Christianity while the rich held onto the more traditional Roman religion. There are numerous reasons for this, but it is partly because the tenets of Christianity appealed to the poor's need for community support. The concept of salvation, the morality of poverty, and the vindication of the meek caught on in a way that it did not for the upper classes. The seasons impact the poor much more than the rich, and several cultural seasonal traditions that celebrated the return of the spring began as practises amongst the poor, not the rich. Similarly, these traditions often endured as folk practices among the poor even after they fell out of formal religious observance in the rest of society.

Different classes will have different vocabularies and use different metaphors and similes that draw on imagery that arises from the pressures in their lives. A king may liken something being plentiful to a banquet where a peasant likens it to a bountiful harvest. Following the Battle of Hastings in 1066, much of the upper class in England became French speakers. This only

---

[34] Laura McClure *Spoken Like a Woman: Speech and Gender in Athenian Drama* (Princeton University Press, United States, 2009)

slowly trickled down the poor, who slowly absorbed the French phrases and words that we use today.

Summary

1. Though wealth, power, and status correlate, they can still be distributed differently across the class system because they come from different places. Figure out what your society culturally values for status, materially values for wealth, and how one exercises power.

2. The distribution of wealth, power, and status is often out of sync as society changes. Consider how societal understandings of these things that define class are changing at the time of your story.

3. Consider which things make social mobility easier—either going up or down—like technology, education, magic, genetics, skills, the military, prejudice, religious ideals, cultural norms, or legal barriers.

4. Caste systems are usually based on immutable characteristics and make social mobility harder, but they do not necessarily have to be oppressive in fictional alien or non-human societies. The line between class and caste systems is not as defined as we like to think, especially with regard to 'untouchables'.

5. Culture will differ from class to class: what people eat, do for fun, what they wear, what they say, how they say it, their religion, morals, traditions, and social norms. These will be influenced by different forces in their lives. Education, trade, and technology can all undermine the lines between these cultures, and thus the lines between classes.

HOW CLASS SYSTEMS ARE MAINTAINED

The Hunger Games by Suzanne Collins
The Handmaid's Tale by Margaret Atwood
The Great Gatsby by F Scott Fitzgerald
Do Androids Dream of Electric Sheep by Philip K Dick
The Legend of Korra created by Mike DiMartino and Bryan Koientzko
The Belgariad by David Eddings
Breach of Peace by Daniel B Greene
Dune by Frank Herbert

Class and caste systems are an important part of the way societies have worked for a long time in the sense that they have been (and still are) powerful shapers of our world. This chapter will be split into four parts: maintaining a class structure, the rich and powerful, class systems are not static things, and the origins of class.

Maintaining a class structure

Class systems are like any other sociological structure: they must be maintained, consciously and unconsciously, otherwise they will change or fall apart. It is easy to think of these systems in terms of the oppressor and the oppressed, but this is almost always overly simplistic.[35] Not because class systems cannot be oppressive, but because the two greatest reasons class and caste systems persist, even if they are oppressive, are:

1. People believe in the way the system works.
2. People do not see any issue with the oppression—and in fact regard it as reasonable, moral, or necessary.

Class systems like Panem in *The Hunger Games*, where there is an overwhelming social divide almost purely based on fear are, on average, a lot more fragile. The system does not encourage passivity or acceptance of the way it works. The brutal repression of the Thirteen Districts only ever fostered rebellion by sending their children to die every year in televised sport. Suzanne Collins seemed to realise how fragile this brutal system was, which is partly why the Capitol fell apart with little real resistance in *Mockingjay*—it was held together scotch tape and willpower and not much else.

The exception to this in Panem's worldbuilding is District One, which shared a broadly profitable relationship with the Capitol. They benefitted from the class system to the extent that life was mostly pleasant, and they had come to see competing in the Hunger Games as a source of pride, ambition, and glory. That is, they did not see any issue with the oppression and believed the Games were reasonable. It is not surprising the class system persisted in District One with relative ease.

Class systems where large swathes of the population do not believe in the way it works can persist for a long time. The slave states of the United States of America and the Caribbean French colonies were a brutal dystopia for the African slaves forcibly transported there, and they continued for hundreds of years, but these were contingent on a large non-slave population. Where *The Hunger Games* saw the Capitol outnumbered ten to

---

[35] It is as if millions of Marxists suddenly cried out in terror and were suddenly silenced.

one by those they oppressed, white Americans outnumbered slaves in the south almost two to one.

This is partly why caste systems have been so persistent. They bring with them a strong moral belief about why people should be divided the way they are—some people deserving more, others deserving less. Questioning the caste system becomes questioning society's moral values, scripture, or even questioning God himself. If you can make an objective moral imperative for oppressing another group, not only are the oppressor *and* oppressed less likely to question the state of society, but there is an immaterial and psychological benefit to perpetuating the harm. It can even be explicitly seen as a moral good.

While this *can* happen in class structures too—for example, people might believe a society is a strict capitalistic meritocracy when it is not—it is usually less explicit, with no creed or scripture to point to. These values and social paradigms are in constant flux, shifting and changing with no canonical answer.

It is a powerful thing to believe that while you are not the wealthiest or most powerful, things are *fine*, right? Or that the people who do have it all probably deserve it, or that things will get better eventually if you keep working, so there is no need to overturn society. This is especially the case when a population does not see the exploitation or repression at the foundations of a caste or class society. People at the top and bottom will often have delusional ideas about how the system 'really works' that fools them into thinking everyone is having a good (enough) time.

A Martin Luther King Jr. quote is quite relevant here:

'I have almost reached the regrettable conclusion that [our] great stumbling block in the stride toward freedom is not the… Ku Klux Klanner, but the white moderate who is more devoted to 'order' than to justice; who prefers a negative peace which is the absence of tension to a positive peace which is the presence of justice...'[36]

The unaffected, apathetic, unknowledgeable, ignorant, or uncaring are a powerful force in maintaining a system like this. Does the class structure in your worldbuilding have a 'white moderate'? Consider how people believing in your system and people not caring or knowing about its problems may play into how your system is maintained, both passively and actively.

<u>The rich and powerful</u>

While the rich and powerful may not be sitting around in dark rooms, smoking cigars, and talking about how they can wring another dollar from the neck of the working man, they will, on average, act in their own interests, usually reinforcing the system. How they vote, who they donate to, which bills they lobby for in a democracy.

Slave-owners in the United States lobbied to pass the Fugitive Slave Act of 1850 which required slaves to be returned to their owner even if they managed to escape to a free state. It also passively encouraged and justified kidnappings of black persons, as well as making the Federal government responsible for following up on escaped slaves. This burden of responsibility reinforced the slave hierarchy in the United States, and it was largely orchestrated by the rich and powerful.

In India, there was a massive campaign by those of the highest caste to ban marriage across caste lines when they realised that it was causing a decline in the caste system's influence, threatening their position.

The 250-year-long Conflict of the Orders from 500 to 287 BC was an era long struggle for the lower-class plebeians of Roman society to finally gain similar rights to the upper-class

---

[36] Letter from Martin Luther King Jr. *Letter from Birmingham Jail* regarding the civil rights movement (16 April 1963)

patricians. The patricians fought it every step of the way to preserve the order as they knew it.

In each of these cases, the rich and powerful used the law to maintain the class structure as they knew it. But there are perhaps even more pervasive strategies they have used to reinforce these structures. You may wish to use some of these in your worldbuilding:

1. Legal barriers to social mobility → In Margaret Atwood's *The Handmaid's Tale,* the Wives and Commanders represent a tiny subset of the Republic of Gilead, but entering their privileged circles means prior approval from the Commanders themselves and evidence of religious devotion. There is no social ladder to climb with wealth or fame in Gilead, and people who do not conform to their religious expectations are not legally permitted to rise in the Republic.

2. Cultural barriers and social norms that exclude those who do not understand them → *The Great Gatsby* explores this in detail. Entering the 'upper class' is not simply a question of wealth or power, but a complicated series of mannerisms, assumptions, clothing choices, and pastimes. Not only does Nick Carraway feel like he cannot pass these cultural barriers, but Gatsby himself spent years performing these things in hopes of truly entering the 'upper class'. Not conforming can lead to being ostracised.

3. Cronyism → Appointing friends and associates to positions of authority without truly considering their qualifications. Job promotions and political advancement are vital for social mobility, but cronyism acts as a barrier—often one that is never openly acknowledged but can very clearly be felt by those on the 'outside'.

4. Economic monopolies → Philip K Dick's *Do Androids Dream of Electric Sheep* is set in a corporate dystopia. The class system rigidly divides the wealthy from the poor with little chance for social mobility. The poor are stuck in cycles of poverty sustained by subscriptions to corporations and the inability to ever gather enough capital to become independent from them. The Rosen Association has a near-monopoly on high-end android manufacturing, and with androids becoming such a vital part of everyday life, it passively reinforces the class system by keeping important sources of capital in the hands of a few.

5. Artificial scarcity of resources → Closely linked to economic monopolies, artificial scarcity allows the powerful to control who has access to what resources and materials. This access can influence who is socially mobile, who can exercise power in society, and the quality of life someone enjoys.

6. Making less powerful individuals dependent on them for money, status, or wealth → During the American Civil War, 40,000 Irish Americans fought for the Confederacy. At the time, the Irish did not have the status of being truly 'white' in the United States, similar to how Slavic populations in Europe were looked down upon as not truly 'European'. The Confederacy persuaded them to join the effort to preserve the institution of slavery under the guise of white camaraderie and suggested that by fighting with them, they might secure equal social status as whites.[37] This slave-driven class system was preserved for a time by making the Irish dependent on southern white Americans for status, money, and power. These things

---

[37] David T Gleeson *The Green and the Gray: The Irish in the Confederate States of America* (University of North Carolina Press, United Stated, 2016)

could be taken away as easily as they could be given. We discussed in the chapter on monarchies how Queen Elizabeth I used the patronage system to retain her power and influence by making the nobles dependent on her for their own power, wealth, and status. It is worth considering who gives who power, wealth, and status in your society. What are their motives, and how easy is it to attain these things without their support or approval?

7. Meaningless concessions → Perhaps your society is in a state of social upheaval. One way to quell this is with symbols and promises of change that never amount to much at all. A statue dedicated to the 'struggle for liberation' while never pursuing deeper legal rights for the oppressed.

8. Propaganda → In *The Legend of Korra*, the city of Ba Sing Se is profoundly unequal. The city itself is divided into the inner, middle, and outer rings with the wealth, power, and status almost exclusively lying in the hands of those in the inner. The writers went out of their way to show how this system persists in the face of overwhelming inequality. Over generations, the poorest in the city have been fed propaganda that the royal family is infinitely wise and deserving of all they now enjoy. As one character's house burns down, she goes back to rescue her picture of the queen. There is a propagandistic religious reverence to the class structure that helps maintain the system. People have been wrongly convinced that Ba Sing Se is a meritocracy of sorts with the wisest and most capable holding all the power and wealth.

It may be worth picking a few of these and experimenting with how they support the system in your society, or even how the lack or failure of one may be undermining it.

In the previous chapter, we discussed social mobility and how particular groups will be more socially mobile than others. Magic and technology can radically challenge and subvert the traditional barriers to social mobility, making whole demographics more mobile than they ever were before. The question becomes: how do the rich and powerful either incentivise this group to reinforce the class structure or what extra barriers do they create to prevent them from undermining it?

In the *Shadow and Bone* series, the countries of Shu Han and Fjerda both persecute the grisha—a class of magical people. In other words, they place extreme barriers to them ever attaining power, wealth, or status in hopes of maintaining the social order as they know it. In contrast, the state of Ravka incentivises them to act in Ravka's interest by giving them power and status in the army. There is something of a symbiotic relationship at play; the elites in Ravka incorporate the grisha into the class system, allowing it to change, but on their terms.

<u>Class systems are not static things</u>

One common mistake worldbuilders make is that they show how a caste or class system may have *originated* in their world, with a thorough understanding of the psychology and beliefs behind it, but the system itself *never changes*. It persists, sometimes for even thousands of years in a pure form, unchanged and unchallenged. The truth is these power structures are constantly changing—how they define status and power, which resources they value, which groups are accepted and stigmatised, which conflicts dominate the social dialogue. The present decides society as much as history.

> 'The fact is that even in traditional times, the caste system never existed as it was theoretically supposed to operate… My family belongs to the ancient Syrian Christian Community of Kerala…

the Syrian Christians were given a high status in the
caste system, even though, strictly speaking, the
caste system applies only to Hindus.'
— Dr Abraham Thomas[38]

The Indian caste system was radically changed by British
colonisation in 1881. The British, themselves a class-bound
society, re-organised Indian society, making the caste system
firmer in many ways than it ever had been before. It was
codified into law largely because it was viewed as a method of
control. Just as class systems shape society, they too are shaped
by their social environment. By the economics, religions, and
political realities that shift the lens through which we might
understand a caste system. Even caste systems with rigid rules
need to accommodate sociological and demographic change or
risk collapse. Keeping your worldbuilding the same over such
long stretches of time makes your society, and even your
characters within it, implausible and stagnant.

The truth is, status is often defined by those who already
have status, whether they realise it or not. People from non-
Western countries learn English because it is the language of the
wealthy nowadays. Following the 1066 Battle of Hastings, a new
Norman-French upper class took power in the British Isles, and
as a result, people who wished to climb the social ladder had to
learn French.

In a self-sustaining feedback loop, your wealthy, powerful,
and positioned will define what it takes to be wealthy, powerful,
and positioned.

The origins of class

---

[38] Dr Abraham V Thomas "Is There a Caste System in India?" (1984) 2
Bridgewater Review Article 7

Historians and anthropologists Professors Melvin
Kranzburg and Michael T Hannan proposed the following
theory for the origins of class structure:

> 'Communal activity [to organise and harvest
> more food and material in larger groups] had
> important social implications. Food had to be
> equitably distributed, and a leader was needed to
> organize and direct the group. Because the basic
> social group was the family tribe, kin
> relationships—from the tribal chief down—formed
> the basis for the "managerial hierarchy."... [By] the
> time written history began, distinct economic and
> social classes were in existence, with members of
> each class occupying a certain place in the
> organization of work. At the apex of the social
> pyramid stood the ruler... and the nobles... Closely
> aligned with them were the priests; possessing
> knowledge of writing and mathematics, the priests
> served as government officials, organizing and
> directing the economy and overseeing clerks and
> scribes.'[39]

These are broad guidelines, and not hugely helpful when
worldbuilding beyond a very basic pre-agrarian society. What is
worth noting is while the 'managerial hierarchy' has changed
since its initial conception, class systems today remain intimately
linked to the ownership, management, and control of resources.
It is at least worth examining that relationship within your
worldbuilding.

It does, however, reveal three questions that might prompt
deeper worldbuilding. What originally caused people to live in
larger groups? Which resources were they attempting to gather

---

[39] Prof. Melvin Kranzburg and Michael T Hannan "History of the
organisation of work" (Britannica)

more efficiently? What religious or philosophical beliefs
influenced the class structure?

Perhaps the gods are heavily involved in your world,
prompting people to organise around their divine leadership. In
Daniel B Greene's *Breach of Peace,* the Empire is headed by the
Almighty—a divine figure who bestows great power on their
disciples, the Anointed. Perhaps instead of food, they needed to
cooperate to harvest a special resource like the spice melange
from Frank Herbert's *Dune.* Though we do not know how the
indigenous Fremen society arose originally in that world, it is
not beyond belief that they formed around a need to harvest the
spice—this miraculous resource that bestows superior mental
faculties.

Magic might significantly impact how your classes form by
changing who is powerful and what status means. To continue
with our *Dune* example, the Faufreluche system in Frank
Herbert's *Dune* series is feudalistic—based around tiers of lords,
nobles, and dukes beneath an Emperor—but it evolved to
accommodate the Bene Gesserit, a sect of women with powerful
magical abilities. Where it would have likely otherwise been
dominated by men, the Great Houses seek to use the Bene
Gesserit as wives and consultants as they compete with one
another economically and politically. This is also why the
Emperor almost always has a Bene Gesserit wife. They are vital
strategic investments. The Bene Gesserit are a powerful faction
on their own, eventually revealed to have been manipulating
events for hundreds of years.

Class and caste systems are also often linked to historic
conflicts between groups—ethnic, cultural, religious, and
otherwise. Caste systems evolve along similar guidelines but
tend to place a special emphasis on the religious element. The
Hindu Rigveda divides society into four groups morally
destined for their position.

The Indian caste system can theoretically be traced back to
divisions and conflicts between Vedic tribes. The arrival of the

Indo-Iranians played into those tribal conflicts, but they brought with them a 'particular principle of social ordering called Varna… which was based on the four hierarchical divisions of function in society… Skin colour was an important indicator in determining an individual's caste.'[40] A long-term consequence of this was that those historic conflicts informed how the caste system arose in the first place, with ethnic tensions, loyalties, victories and losses influencing who ended up where. Class divides were not just determined by the organisation of labour, but the national historical narrative.

Summary

1. Class structures are most securely maintained by a majority believing in the way the society works or not seeing any issue with oppression. Systems based purely on fear are more fragile. This is also why caste systems are persistent.
2. Class systems are self-reinforcing paradigms partly regulated by those who already have wealth, status and power, consciously and unconsciously through legal and cultural barriers, cronyism, dependency, violence, ostracism, monopolies, artificial scarcity, propaganda, meaningless concessions, and elsewise.
3. Though a class system may begin with a certain geopolitical, sociological, religious, or belief set-up, these things will change the longer the class or caste system persists. Keeping it the same makes your world feel stagnant. They need to adapt to accommodate sociological and demographic changes over time.
4. Social mobility is fundamentally about where the incentives and barriers in your society. Consider how

---

[40] Manali S Deshpande "History of the Indian Caste System and its Impact on India Today" (Phd, California Polytechnic State University, 2010)

magic and technology change or remove these incentives and barriers for some groups, as well as how the rich and powerful respond to new technologies and magic that might challenge the system as it is.

5. Class systems arose initially because of people living in larger groups, the organisation of labour, conflict between groups, and belief systems. Caste systems tend to put more emphasis on belief systems. Magic will significantly change the reasons behind these things.

HOW CLASS SYSTEMS COLLAPSE

The Elder Scrolls series developed by Bethesda Studios
The Lies of Locke Lamora by Scott Lynch
A Tale of Two Cities by Charles Dickens
A Storm of Swords by GRR Martin
Mockingjay by Suzanne Collins
Dune by Frank Herbert
The Lord of the Rings by JRR Tolkien

Fiction is often about radical change in the social order, especially in science fiction and fantasy, which commonly play with war, revolution, and conspiracy. How class or caste systems change, collapse, and degenerate will necessarily be a part of this. This chapter will be split into five sections: peaceful change, violent change, what happens after class, plague, and war.

<u>Peaceful change</u>

Class systems can change or end when the barriers to class mobility significantly lower, making people far more socially mobile. It is worth noting here that 'change' in the social order is not necessarily positive, but the system as it stands may cease to exist. For one example from Ancient China:

> '… the competitive civil-service examination
> system… for the recruitment of the members of the

ruling class... accounted for the decline of the pre-Tang and early Tang aristocracy.'[41]

The Chinese examination system made it radically easier for people outside the noble class to acquire power, status, and then wealth. It was a largely peaceful transition with the hegemony of the day breaking down because the barriers to social mobility were undermined by this new political-religious philosophy. The decline of the old aristocracy saw a shift in the social order.

Guilds and unions have been important players in breaking down, changing, or even reinforcing barriers to social mobility. *The Elder Scrolls* is a game series with some truly unique worldbuilding, partly in how it uses guilds to inform its social landscape. The emergence of the Fighters Guild as an organisation open to anyone, rich and poor, who can prove themselves lent power, wealth, and status to laymen in a feudalistic system where they would otherwise not have it. It presented a challenge to the traditional power structures in Tamriel by creating a new social ladder to climb. It also meant there was a significant body of fighters independent of the noble class. This influence manifested in members having legal exemptions for weapons, demanding higher pay for their work, and acquiring a status they could not previously enjoy.

Unions have consistently used their control over significant portions of the economy to pressure the government into better pay and working conditions. The health and safety reforms of the early twentieth century, as well as the substantial wage increases, were in part the result of unions negotiating on behalf of their members. Unions and guilds have a measurable impact on the distribution of and ways to acquire power, wealth, and status. As a result, they often face opposition.

---

[41] Pang-Ti Ho "Aspects of Social Mobility in China, 1368-1911" (1959) 1 CSSH 330

However, guilds and unions have also restricted the social mobility of others at times. Consider this passage from *The Lies of Locke Lamora* by Scott Lynch, which alludes to how guilds can become powerful and manipulative:

> 'One night a powerful sorcerer knocks on the door of a less-powerful sorcerer. "I'm starting an exclusive guild," he says. "Join me now or I'll blast you out of your fucking boots right where you stand." So naturally the second mage says…
> "You know, I've always wanted to join a guild!"
> Right. Those two go bother a third sorcerer. "Join the guild," they say, "or fight both of us, two on one, right here and right now." Repeat as necessary, until three or four hundred guild members are knocking on the door of the last independent mage around, and everyone who said no is dead.'

Independent workers can sometimes get in the way of what guilds and unions are trying to accomplish. Consequently, there have been instances where they have punished those who decline to join them by making it difficult to get hired, demand exclusive relationships with clients, or driving them out of business in order to maintain an effective monopoly. During the Ventian Renaissance of the sixteenth and seventeenth centuries, the Venetian guilds exercised a huge amount of power over the politics of the city by doing this, creating a top-down hierarchy of craftsman that did not always work to benefit all.

Unions have, at times, demanded pay or power that the economy either cannot handle or would not see a reasonable return on. In any given society, guilds and unions will be a complicated mix of all these things—beneficial and manipulative, overbearing and liberating, ambitious and not ambitious enough. A union might be bad for one class and good for another; a guild might undermine one class and grow another. It is up to you to find the balance that fits best with your world.

Sometimes, the beliefs that underpin a class system may peacefully change or fall away. Government programs in both Japan and India working to help the lower castes—who have been historically discriminated against—reflect a changing belief in the validity of these caste systems. Over time, it works to dismantle the system itself. Even in 1984, Dr Abraham Thomas wrote:

> 'Does caste exist in India? Sure it does. But… not the same as it was two hundred or one hundred or even twenty years ago.'[42]

We discussed in the previous chapter that class systems are not static things; that they often change as the beliefs that underpin them change. We discussed how previously we valued inherited wealth, and even saw it as a valid and moral source of status and power, but that people have come to emphasise acquired wealth—especially as economic and political tensions have risen over the last few decades. Work ethic and productivity have become supreme virtues that underpin how we understand who deserves power, wealth, and status, and because of that, who gets it. Consequently, policies like inheritance taxes have entered the social conversation more and more.

<u>Violent changes</u>

Why have healthy gradual social change when you can have blood? Revolution or civil war happen for a myriad of reasons, but here we will only focus on the class-related aspects.

---

[42] Dr Abraham V Thomas "Is There a Caste System in India?" (1984) 2 Bridgewater Review Article 7

Class tensions act as major internal economic and political forces in society, so it is no surprise that almost every major civil war and revolution in history has been underpinned by them to some extent. It is common and tempting to write stories where revolutions and wars are waged for pure idealistic reasons — truth, hope, justice, the American Way — and that those alone are enough to keep people fighting. The reality is not only that these ideas are nearly always more complicated than presented in such stories, but that wars and revolutions are usually motivated by more grounded things.

The revolutionaries in the 1917 Russian Revolution may insist that it succeeded because of their fervent belief in social equity, freedom, justice, and equality, but its slogan was 'Peace, Bread, and Land'. People wanted out of the gruesome First World War that had killed millions of their countrymen, they wanted food when they were hungry, and they wanted a place to live and call their own. Even if your main characters are purely motivated by idealism, most people will get behind a revolution or civil war for these more grounded reasons. An inspirational speech only goes so far, and seeing the poor countrymen of your world throw stable, well-fed lives away for abstract concepts is a little melodramatic.

Charles Dickens' *A Tale of Two Cities* takes place in the lead up to the French Revolution, which the revolutionaries might argue was founded on truth, justice, and egalitarianism. Certainly, if you looked at the propaganda that followed, you might walk away with this impression. However, Dickens worked hard to portray the exploitation and interference the poor faced at the hands of the ruling class more than he ever did their concern for high-minded concepts. One of the most famous scenes in the novel is a clear metaphor: Dickens has a French nobleman order his carriage recklessly driven through streets filled with the poor when it accidentally hits and kills a child, and he leaves only a gold coin in compensation. The rich recklessly interfere in the lives of the poor, and the poor die for it. As you read *A Tale of Two Cities*, you are left with a distinct understanding that the poor do not lead stable, ordered, safe lives, and that these things matter more. Justice and truth can wait.

After class?

Littlefinger was right when he said chaos is a ladder. In GRR Martin's *A Storm of Swords*, Daenerys overthrows the slave-driven class system of Astapor. Chaos springs up in its wake. Though Daenerys sets up a council to rule the city with a newly established semi-egalitarian class system, it collapses almost immediately. A group of ex-slaves forcefully take power and establish a new order of their own, redistributing the resources and land available and putting the masters to death. A new class system will often form out of the remnants of the last, especially if there is chaos or violence involved — the dynamics and impacts of the last class system are not forgotten, and this is often borne out in the social interactions of the new one.

Class is not just an idea. Class is the realistic present distribution of resources, opportunities, and social standing. Revolutions have a complicated track record of realising their ideals, and the people to lead a revolution are not necessarily those best equipped to lead a newly formed government. What happens when the revolutionary fervour that kept the revolutionary factions together dies away? This is also a fascinating place for a story; a post-revolution society trying to implement the ideals that have been fought for. One of the things that Suzanne Collins did quite well in *Mockingjay* was understand that though the rebellion was founded on promoting democracy and equality, the leader of the rebellion, President Coin, was not the sort to relinquish power, and the bloodthirsty rebels would struggle to not take vengeance on the Capitol — even on their children. A significant group voted to create a new Hunger Games as penance.

You can look at it from the perspective of people who suddenly find themselves with wealth and status where they did not have it before, or from the perspective of someone who finds themselves stripped of power and wealth, reduced to nothing. Post-revolution, who controls the infrastructure, the education system, the tax collection, the food and water supplies? How might this affect the transition towards a new society?

Class systems are rarely overturned so absolutely that nothing of them remains in the system that follows. Class is the complex web of social interactions we have with people, and our relationships and sense of self are not so easily overturned. They cannot be overturned with a vote. Who we associate with, who we defer to, who we look down on, and who we identify with are all part of it. These sentiments do not simply vanish overnight.

While they can be deconstructed, remnants of them will often pass into the social web of the system that follows. Frank Herbert's *Dune* series sees the fall of the Faufreluche feudalistic system as the Emperor's line is replaced and Paul Atreides ascends to the throne of the Imperium. He replaces it with a more centralised system of control, but it retains titles like lord, viceroy, and duke, even if what those titles mean and the status and power they command has changed. Our modern class systems are full of similar leftovers from the past. The question for you as a worldbuilder is this: what class systems did your society go through in the past, and how is that reflected linguistically, socially, and economically now?

Plague

The Black Plague from 1346 to 1352 wiped out a substantial portion of the world population, including a third of Europe. It was primarily the peasantry that suffered these losses, not having the wealth or resources to isolate themselves from the onslaught. Tolkien was acutely aware of this and wrote about how his Great Plague was, 'greater in Rhovanion [which] had no great cities… [its people] were little skilled in the arts of healing and medicine.' Rhovanion had always been impoverished compared to states like Gondor and Rohan.

One consequence of the Black Plague, and likely the Great Plague of Middle Earth, was a labour shortage left in its wake. Peasants were rarer and less expendable as a workforce than they ever were before. This allowed them to demand greater pay and portions of the crops they yielded, as well as more rights and respect. Power, wealth, and status.

The English nobility resisted this at every turn, enacting the Statute of Labourers in 1351 to prohibit demanding higher wages than pre-plague standards, but the economic and social pressures triumphed over time with the end of the feudal system as they knew it. Plague can shift the economic value of the demographics that suffer.

<u>War</u>

In war, people—shockingly—die. World War I had huge consequences for class structures across Europe. Part-timers, casual labourers, and the unemployed could suddenly earn good money and feed themselves after the war. In Britain, women became an employed class in factories and shops to help the war effort, and it meant they demanded the vote—power.

Even so, the relationship between class and war is highly dependent on several other factors: the popularity of the war, casualties, length, a sense of victory or defeat, toll on the remaining civilians not in service, strain on the economy, and many other things. Professor Gerald Jordan writes:

> '… conscription and the direction of labour made for a more inclusive sense of national identity [in 1914 Britain]… Nationalism was one legacy of the war… Although war sensitised workers to class inequality… nationalist sentiments in popular

culture set limits on the political consequences of class feeling.'[43]

War can give a cultural sense of purpose to inequalities, creating a bigger picture to fight for and thus shelving class issues, but it can also exacerbate and expose those same issues. In 1917 Russia, long work hours and costs of living were already a crippling issue in the empire, and they were only made worse by the demands of the war. The Bolsheviks capitalised on this and promised 'Peace, Bread, and Land', revolting and taking over. They ended Russia's involvement in the First World War with the Treaty of Brest-Litovsk. When you strip away the facade of idealism, people just want to go home.

Both class and war are so complicated that saying they interact in one specific way would be unhelpful. Even so, it is worth recognising that they interact in your worldbuilding. Just how they do that is up to you.

Summary

1. Class systems can change peacefully. Sometimes, the barriers to social mobility will naturally lower, and other times the beliefs underpinning the distribution of wealth, power, and status will shift. Guilds and unions can be important players in causing or preventing this kind of change.
2. However idealistic your heroes might be, consider the economic and social tensions that underpin both sides of a conflict.
3. The post-revolution and post-war scenario are difficult to navigate and will not always result in peace and prosperity. What happens when the winning side no longer has a single enemy to face? Who controls the resources, infrastructure, and military in this new

---

[43] Gerald Jordan *Comptes Rendus* on 'A Class Society at War: England 1914-18' (York University Press, United Kingdom, 2010)

society? This will often influence the new distribution of wealth, power, and status.

4. Class systems may change but remnants of them will remain. Consider how past class systems are still reflected in language, organisations, political structures, and otherwise.

5. Plague and war have played important roles in intensifying and nullifying class struggles. Labour shortages can lead to a higher quality of life for the survivors, while war can give a unifying sense of purpose that obscures class struggles. It can also exacerbate them.

CITIES AND TOWNS

A Song of Ice and Fire by GRR Martin
The Lord of the Rings by JRR Tolkien
Speaker for the Dead by Orson Scott Card
The Stormlight Archives by Brandon Sanderson
The Elder Scrolls series developed by Bethesda Studios
Children of Time Adrian Tchaikovsky
Valerian and the City of a Thousand Planets directed by Luc Besson
Dune by Frank Herbert

You want your characters to travel through an immersive world full of colourful but realistic towns and cities. Where should you put them on your map? Settlements, towns, and cities have sprung up for different reasons across history as different economic, political, religious, and social forces demand different things. In this chapter, we will move through history from the ancient era to the modern era to look at some of the many reasons cities have sprung up and collapsed, and how they might apply to your fictional world.

The Ancient Era

Chief among the reasons our first cities grew was agriculture—an exercise requiring a permanent location with large numbers of people for the harvest. In worldbuilding Westeros, the primary setting for *A Song of Ice and Fire*, GRR Martin gave thought to the agriculture that the continent's oldest city would be built on. Oldtown was built around a broad freshwater river that created some of the most fertile land on the continent, capable of easily supporting crop harvests, even through hard seasons. The Reach is regularly referred to as the 'the breadbasket of the Seven Kingdoms' for this reason.

Agricultural technology meant that a population could produce more food than they would by hunting and gathering, but it required that they remain in the same place—both to tend to the crop throughout the year and defend it from others. This partly explains why our first cities emerged in the Fertile Crescent and southern China where some of Earth's most fertile land could be found, along with predictable supplies of fresh water. This is also why human settlements have nearly always grown around rivers—like Oldtown did—or lakes. The question for you as a worldbuilder is where the fertile land and fresh water was in your world when civilisation first grew.

A second element to consider is the systemic organisation of work. This is where society changes from everyone gathering food and water to a society with a labouring class and a managerial class to direct that labour—usually because larger food and water sources require planning to maximise output. This is partly why irrigation projects along the Nile and in Mesopotamia were crucial to city development in those regions. Anyone can farm, but it takes a massive group of people to properly develop irrigation and maximise the harvest that comes from it. This creates a population centre that evolves into what we now call a city.

For a fictional example, consider JRR Tolkien's Osgiliath. Osgiliath was the original capital of Gondor in Middle Earth for over a thousand years before its fall. It was bigger than Minas Tirith, being built on a freshwater river with a lot more space for agriculture and housing. It was the natural place for Gondor's largest city to grow until plague and war led to a mass exodus. People fled to the far more defensible Minas Tirith, backed against a mountain with high walls, and it became Gondor's new capital.

Important religious and cultural sites also draw large populations together, even if only temporarily, for festivals and traditions. The original capital of Japan, Kyoto, supposedly sprung up around the Shimogamo Shrine, which people would often make pilgrimages to as a form of imperial patronage. Its location was partly chosen for religious reasons: the northern mountain border could protect the city from evil spirits. This link between the religious and the political gave rise to a city. In time, the capital of Japan moved across the country to better reflect the centres of trade and power, but it goes to show the influence religious places can have. Which sites have symbolic or historic ritualistic importance to the populations in your world, and how do they inform how a city is designed and built? It was very common for government and religion to be one and the same in the ancient world, so political centralisation often aligned with religious sites.

But perhaps your fictional species of elves or aliens works entirely differently, leading to different justifications for city-building. In Orson Scott Card's *Speaker for the Dead*, the pequeninos are small pig-like creatures, and over the course of the story, their culture and social structure are studied by a colony of scientists. In time, the reader learns that the pequeninos naturally evolved in cities because of how their life cycle works. When they 'die', they become trees which help fertilise and produce their young, providing guidance and materials for housing in their society. They were not first motivated by agriculture to congregate but rather because they needed to stay together near their trees to reproduce. It is worth noting that the story does explore how agriculture helps one society grow ten times larger than the rest into the greatest city on the planet, but this is a species that was already naturally inclined to congregate in large numbers—it just helped those numbers grow quicker.

If your fictional species does not use agriculture like humans, figure out which primal concerns they would have that might make them come together: sustenance, reproduction, defence against predators, and so on.

In Frank Herbert's *Dune*, the city of Arrakeen was built around harvesting the spice, which was essential for space trade, space travel, and asserting power in the galaxy. It was also built around a massive aquifer due to water scarcity on the planet.

Even so, this is dealing with the ancient era and how cities first formed. While some stories like *Children of Time* or *Children of Ruin* by Adrian Tchaikovsky deal with the ascent of civilisations over thousands of years, most science fiction and fantasy takes place in a more advanced time. One mistake I commonly see is that the greatest cities ever built in a world have always been the greatest city, and that no cities have ever died out, nor have their populations ever moved on. Our world is full of ruins and depopulated cities that were once centres of politics in countries that no longer exist, trading for things we no longer need, founded on religions that have long died. The centres of your world will change over time.

The pre-industrial era

Moving on to the narrow field of discussion known as all human history, new reasons for cities have come along as human needs have changed, the most important of which is trade. Humans soon realised that rivers, lakes, and seas like the Mediterranean or Black could help them exchange goods quicker and safely. As a result, cities—as the nodes of trade across the world—became a way to increase your standard of living. More people to sell to and buy from meant more was to be made.

In Brandon Sanderson's *The Stormlight Archives*, Kharbranth is a trade city on the coast, and allowing shipments to pass through with little question keeps it wealthy. But perhaps your world has no rivers or lakes, or its freshwater is only found in aquifers, as in *Dune's* Arrakis, or it has a faster method of travel than via boat. In which case, the machinery of trade may work slightly differently, influencing where 'trade cities' pop up in your world. To continue with *The Stormlight Archives* as an example, Kharbranth not only thrived because of its trade capacity, but because it is positioned to survive the vicious high storms that ravage the continent—wedged between two cliff-faces. Places that would be great for trade are not necessarily safe against the high storms. Likewise, places vulnerable to attack or disaster may not become trade cities.

Major routes between key cities often end up littered with trade posts as well, capitalising on the traffic. As the Silk Road became more popular, towns like Kashgar and Merv thrived as they capitalised on large swathes of people reliably moving through the region. This is where GRR Martin may have overlooked one element of his worldbuilding in Westeros. The Kingsroad is a major trade route travelling from the north to the south of the continent, while the River Road and High Road run from east to west and intersect with it. With all the trade travelling through this intersection at the Trident, one would naturally expect a trade city to have grown there. The small castle of House Darry and the Crossroads Inn are found there, but no major population centre taking advantage of the traffic in both directions. It would arguably be an improvement on Martin's worldbuilding to add one.

A fall line is an imaginary line where two different types of land meet—often foothills and coastal plains with a substantial drop in elevation that creates waterfalls and river rapids. Settlements spring up along fall lines to take advantage of the energy generated by waterfalls to power turbines and to be a transition point for trade moving upstream and onto land. While I do not necessarily advocate going so far as to figure out the tectonic plate movements of your planet, it can be valuable to decide where coastal plains meet foothills or where ancient earthquakes might have caused sharp tectonic shifts that change elevation.

Trade grows in part from specialisation, which is when groups within a population develop more niche, 'specialised' skills: baking, fighting, smithing, and storytelling are some examples. Specialisation leads to a demand for new resources as required for those industries, in turn leading living standards to improve, and people to develop new interests that demand new resources. Kremnica in Slovakia popped up in the ninth century to mine the Kremnica Mountains for gold, a valuable resource as currencies became more common and the demand for jewellery grew. Which materials have come into and fallen out of demand across history, leading to new towns forming in places that harvest them?

City states

Khabranth is the archetypical city state: perfectly situated for trade on the coast with trade between larger cities passing by it, defensible inside a wedge of a canyon and backed by inhospitable mountains. City states need to be isolated enough that the empires of the world do not swallow them up, which is why so many fell during the Colonial Period in our world. Looking at your fictional map, which places are defensible, positioned for trade networking, and away from major powers which might otherwise gobble them up? City states sometimes appear as a result of colonialism as well—one power establishing itself on the land of another—and they can crop up in clusters like the Greek city states or the Hanseatic League.

Political centralisation

In time, humanity started to form states and empires rather than just independent settlements. Karakorum was once the capital of the Mongol Empire, and while it was positioned in a religiously important place, it was also built in the heart of Orkhon Valley—the centre of Mongolian territory. In a time when physical distance was important for efficient governance, both in communication and the capacity to exert force, political centralisation mattered. Constantine moved his capital from Rome to Byzantium following the fall of the Western Roman Empire. With the rise of the Sassanids and the new Persian Empire, as well revolts and unrest in the east, core events in the Empire were happening far from Rome. The Roman Empire had a history of dividing its rule and territory for more efficient governance, but when Constantine unified it in 324, he settled in the place that would be most advantageous for his political centralisation.

Perhaps your civilisation does not require physical proximity to ensure efficient governance. Technology means distance is no longer a factor in delivering commands and messages. Nowadays, trade can travel from one side of the world to the other in under a day. In *The Elder Scrolls* series, the Argonians of Black Marsh are connected telepathically to the Hist—ancient eldritch beings who take the form of trees—who guide and protect them. They warn the Argonians of an invasion from another dimension, which allows them to prepare and fend it off. Because of this telepathic connection, there is not nearly the same need to have a politically centralised city, especially when the Hist are spread out across the region. Settlements spring up around their groves, rather than the places we have discussed previously. As a result, Black Marsh is the only region on the continent without a clear capital that carries the political weight and population that the rest do.

In your world, maybe long and terrible season changes force people to migrate every hundred years, or the continents are based around the bodies of fallen gods, and so cities grow around major body parts, or maybe your species needs to make pilgrimages to keep their souls from being condemned. Towns would spring up along those pilgrimage paths. You can make your world whatever you want.

The Industrial Era

The Industrial Era has become an increasingly popular setting for fantasy nowadays with authors wanting to move on from the traditional medieval backdrop we know and love. Daniel Greene's *Breach of Peace*, Brandon Sanderson's *Mistborn* series, and Brian McClellan's *The Crimson Campaign* all make use of the industrial forces that overhauled the world in their worldbuilding.

Boomtowns grew like weeds. Coal, gold, iron, and oil propelled the revolution, and towns grew around these resources in the thousands, sometimes overnight. In our day and age, as these resources have dried up or declined in importance, many boomtowns have become ghost towns on the side of the road that you pass in a fleeting glance. Boomtowns were fixtures of the industrial era as much as ghost towns are a fixture of ours. Figure out which resources are propelling your civilisation through an industrial era, where they are found, and which towns have cropped up to harvest them.

Railway towns are similar. These were settlements that sprung up around important rail junctions in a similar way to how towns grew around trade routes. These may connect main cities to boomtowns or boomtowns to other boomtowns. However, the railway is a very specific technology that may not exist in your world. Perhaps there are more or less efficient methods, but the fact remains that towns pop up at junctions people move through, and why and where they move will change across time.

One of the most enduring effects of the Industrial Era has been a population shift from rural areas to cities. Not only did this make cities larger in general, it also changed which urban centres grew in size and importance. Where a city's importance used to be about trade and religion, industry and manufacturing took the lead. Cities with rivers running through them grew because they could use the water to power machinery, and cities near to natural resources capitalised on their proximity. Centres of power naturally gravitate towards centres of population, so it may be worth considering just how the web of power in your world changes across this era. Yet, there is nothing to say your fictional world will follow the same patterns as ours.

In Adrian Tchaikovsky's *Children of Time*, the world is run by a civilisation of super-advanced arachnids. They go through an industrial revolution of their own, but they do not rely on electricity and steam power the way humanity did. Instead, they create computers using chemically controlled ants. Fuel and machinery are biological. As a result, cities grew over ant colonies that could be easily manipulated—these were their gold and coal, the key resources of their civilisation. The city of Manchester grew from a small town of 27,000 to nearly 100,000 in just twenty-five years as the industrial revolution took the region by storm, elevating its status to a major city in the United Kingdom.

<u>Beyond the industrial era</u>

Cities that thrive today are not necessarily industrial centres. New York, London, Shanghai, Hong Kong, and Singapore are the 'financial capitals of the world' with globally high living standards, but only Shanghai has a huge manufacturing base at the same time. Nowadays, 'trade' has changed to include the stock market. Prosperous cities have a stock exchange, reputable financial institutions, a strong regulatory and legal system to protect them, and advanced infrastructure.

If we view civilisation as a story of governments becoming more efficient, bigger, and more powerful, which they generally have, then it explains why planned cities on the scale of the Soviet Union and Maoist China only become possible in the post-industrial world. These have sprung up for ideological, economic, and political reasons. It is up to you to decide whether this kind of city has a place in your world.

In the future, anything can happen. It is 2021 at the time of writing this, and COVID-19 has ravaged the world with nearly five million deaths. Lockdowns have forced businesses to move online, decentralising their work, with employees working from home. It is possible that businesses will move permanently away from the office environment we have grown so accustomed to, and it is curious to wonder what this would do to our cities. Massive decentralisation could see a population shift from urban to rural. The internet has become the largest marketplace on Earth, and there is nothing to say it could not expand into something like the Big Market from Luc Besson's *Valerian and the*

City of the Thousand Planets — a wholly digital city people can log in to and shop at.

Why cities change and adapt

When creating cities and deciding where they go in your world, it can be easy to create them in the abstract without an eye for the history that came before. Perhaps you are creating a town during the industrial era that has been built for smelting. It is tempting to find the perfect place — next to an iron mine, a river for turbines, flat land for housing — and assume a city would *have* to pop up there. But perhaps there is already a city nearby that popped up around a wide freshwater river. Not perfectly situated for the iron mine, but what it does have is momentum. It already has money flowing through it, a working population available for industry, and the organisational structures needed to capitalise on those deposits. It is likely that this city would become the manufacturing base even if there is a *technically* better place for it. Humanity is not perfectly efficient; we never have been, we never will be. We adapt and change, and our world is not perfectly rational. Do not fall into the trap of being perfectly rational yourself.

Summary

1. In the ancient era, cities grew from agriculture and the demand for the systemic organisation of work. Sites of cultural and religious importance drew people together and influenced how a city was designed and worked.
2. Trade is a powerful force in controlling where cities grow and how they evolve. Rivers and lakes have created important nodes for trade for humanity, but this may not be the case for a fictional species. Cities form along trade routes and fall lines and lead to specialisation.

3. The industrial era led to boomtowns around key resources with massive population shifts from rural to urban.

4. The future could hold any kind of city as businesses move online and people work from home more. What 'trade' means has changed these days.

5. Do not make the mistake of being perfectly rational in creating cities in the abstract. Humanity adapts and builds on cities and towns that exist more than we start towns out of nothing. Consider where a city might evolve as well as whether a new settlement might pop up.

HARD WORLDBUILDING VERSUS SOFT WORLDBUILDING

Spirited Away directed by Hayao Miyazaki
The Fellowship of the Ring by JRR Tolkien
Nightfall by Isaac Asimov
Marzipan by Aimee Bender
Nausicaä of the Valley of the Wind by Hayao Miyazaki
Castle in the Sky by Hayao Miyazaki
Howl's Moving Castle by Hayao Miyazaki
Kiki's Delivery Service by Hayao Miyazaki
The *Dark Souls* series developed by FromSoftware
Annihilation by Jeff Vandermeer
The *Nier* series developed by Cavia and PlatinumGames
The *Harry Potter* series by JK Rowling

What is it that makes a Studio Ghibli film so enchanting? In part, it is the stunning visuals and beloved characters, but it is also the worlds crafted in Hayao Miyazaki's unique vision. Science fiction writers have long distinguished between hard and soft science fiction while fantasy authors distinguish hard and soft magic systems. I want to expand on these ways we look at these genres by contrasting two different methods for crafting different types of worlds and stories that immerse the reader in different ways. In a step away from the usual style you will find in this book, this is an essay on hard and soft worldbuilding cowritten by myself and Ellie Gordon.

Worldbuilding is not just the act of creating a fictional world in the abstract. It is also about what you consciously choose to convey to the reader or viewer in the text—what *builds* the world in the mind of the reader. At one end of the spectrum, the textbook example of hard worldbuilding is probably JRR Tolkien's *The Lord of the Rings*. Tolkien created his elvish languages with not just random words translated from English, but a whole alphabet, phonetics, grammar, its own syntax. Gondor and Rohan have complex and detailed histories, distinct cultures that have arisen from that history, and Tolkien goes out of his way to communicate that to the reader in the text. *The Fellowship of the Ring* opens with a prologue called 'Concerning Hobbits' where he details the history of how the little peoples came to the Shire, followed by the passage 'Concerning Pipeweed' where he details the role pipeweed has played in Shire culture, which are then in turn followed by a few more passages on the history of Middle Earth. All three books are littered with details about the flora and fauna of the world. Where things can be explained, Tolkien often tries to. The chapter 'The Council of Elrond' spends many pages alluding to important events in Middle Earth's history—the Downfall of Númenor, the rise of the kingdoms of Men, elvish culture compared to that of hobbits—all of which grounds the reader in a belief that this world makes sense.

Hard worldbuilding is about immersing the reader by giving them detailed, logical, and even realistic cultures, languages, geography, history, and elsewise with an eye for how they all work together. It gives the impression of a well-oiled machine, where all things have been accounted for and can be understood. The world feels as real as our own because it has been so consciously thought through. This is the style of worldbuilding you are perhaps most familiar with. It finds its roots in the hard science fiction of Arthur C Clarke, Isaac Asimov, and Robert Heinlein, who penned stories accounting for the real-world science behind space travel, time dilation, and artificial intelligence, among other things. In *Nightfall,* Isaac

Asimov played with the idea of a planet constantly in the view of a sun and what this would do to the inhabitants' understanding of night, the stars, and society. Such planets do exist out in the cosmos. This style of worldbuilding places the reader in a world grounded in its own web of logic, and it works. It allows the reader to visualise the world you have created more easily, as well as encouraging them to buy into the more fantastical elements you introduce.

In the Studio Ghibli film *Spirited Away*, eight million spirits bathe at Yubaba's huge bathhouse in the middle of an endless ocean made by rain with a train running through it like an artery to nowhere. A third of the way into the film, Yubaba detects something terrible. A monolithic spirit with a foul stench arrives and the protagonist Chihiro is told to clean it. She finds what she calls a 'thorn' in its side, and after pulling it out, a mass of disgusting rubbish and rot fills the room. A being they call the River Spirit then emerges from the water, leaving behind gold and a strange bud as payment. The spirits in the bathhouse treat it with great reverence, almost worship-like, before it rushes off.

This scene is filled with subtle worldbuilding, but it is defined by how little Miyazaki tells us. Miyazaki leaves it up to the viewer to imagine and interrogate just why what happens in this scene happens. The River Spirit is only cured when Chihiro pulls out the masses of trash hidden inside it. We imagine a world where spirits are corrupted by the waste of mankind, explaining why the first thing we see pulled out is a bicycle. We can tie this into the fact spirits hate the smell of humans—a major point earlier in the film—which is never truly explained.

Later on, the bud the River Spirit left behind is revealed to have some loosely defined healing power, but no clear logical worldbuilding connection is drawn between the River Spirit and the bud. No explanation is given as to why it works the way it works. We can also infer something about the social structure of this spirit society from how they treat the River Spirit with reverence. No social hierarchy is laid out throughout the story,

but we are left with a deep impression that there is one—that
this society has a depth we do not see. No justification is given
for the bizarre way spirits look and sound, the hopping lantern,
and the setting is all intentionally peculiar and unconventional.
We are given no logic to rationalise all of this.

While some of this can be explained with an
understanding of Japanese Shintoism—a religion that Miyazaki
drew on when creating *Spirited Away*—not everything can be,
and purposefully so. In 2002, an interviewer told Hayao
Miyazaki that: 'What strikes me about *Spirited Away* compared to
your previous films is a real freedom of the author. A feeling that
you can take the film and the story anywhere you wish,
independent of logic, even.' He gave the following reply:

> 'Everybody can make a film with logic. But my
> way is to not use logic… At a certain moment in
> that process, the lid is opened and very different
> ideas and visions are liberated… I [should not]
> handle a scene in a certain way for the sake of the
> audience. For instance, what for me constitutes the
> end of the film, is the scene in which Chihiro takes
> the train all by herself… I remember the first time I
> took the train alone and what my feelings were at
> the time. To bring those feelings across in the scene,
> it was important to not have a view through the
> window of the train, like mountains or a forest…
> because they are so focused on the ride itself. It's
> while working on that scene that I realised that I
> work in a non-conscious way. There are *more
> profound things than simply logic* that guide the
> creation of the story.'[44]

These 'more profound things' are exactly what soft
worldbuilding aims to harness. Miyazaki is known for having an

---

[44] Interview with Hayao Miyazaki, creator of *Spirit Away* (December
2001) transcript provided by Tom Mes of *Midnight Eye*

incredible grasp of the themes and emotional threads behind his stories, and these come through vividly in the worldbuilding. They grip us and never let go.

The massive gaps Miyazaki leaves in the viewer's understanding of the way this world works creates an otherworldly, mysterious, and foreign feeling to the world of *Spirited Away*. Where *The Lord of the Rings* draws us in through explicit depth in the historical, cultural, and political context of Middle Earth, *Spirited Away* has imagined depth that comes from the viewer or reader themselves wanting to know more.

It is a place full of questions. Telling the viewer explicitly just what all of these strange things mean, making the world wholly navigable, would detract from the enchanting, otherworldly feeling of the spirit world, especially when the story is very intentionally framed from the perspective of a ten-year-old child. The feeling of being lost, being 'spirited away', is crucial to the tonal atmosphere of the story. The soft worldbuilding makes the story more immersive by prioritising that atmospheric and character feeling over logic. Miyazaki crafted a world but did so starting with things that create a *feeling* he wants the viewer to experience — one of those 'more profound things'.

If hard worldbuilding leads to a world that immerses us through consciously communicating concrete rules, consistency, and transparency to create a sense of grounded realism and depth, then soft worldbuilding immerses us through consciously using the unknown, flexible rules, and the reader's imaginative involvement.

It is a different kind of consistency: consistency of emotional or thematic experience for the reader. Where hard worldbuilding keys into a cognitive or intellectual logic, soft worldbuilding keys into an emotional or psychological logic. A world filled with things that channel a particular type of experience and include elements that resonate with that experience even if they don't have any real grounding in that first type of logic. It makes sense and feels consistent to us on an experiential level, psychological or emotional—a type of consistency that writers like Tolkien were less concerned with. It founds a world in what Miyazaki here refers to as those 'more profound things'.

Magical realism has been doing this for a long time. In Aimee Bender's short story *Marzipan,* a man wakes up with a hole in his stomach after his father dies—not metaphorically, but a flesh and blood 'hole the size of a soccer ball and it went all the way through'.

It is worth noting that this way of describing worldbuilding is a spectrum, not a binary choice. You as the writer may choose to withhold things for effect or you may choose to not have answers. You may employ hard worldbuilding in some areas of your world and soft worldbuilding in others. As Nebula-sci-fi-winning-author Nancy Kress puts it:

> 'Even the hardest sci-fi involves some speculation
> or else it would not be science fiction.'[45]

The first strength of soft worldbuilding is it arguably gives you more creative freedom. The story world is not constantly justifying itself to the viewer. *Howl's Moving Castle, Spirited Away,* and *Kiki's Delivery Service* could have whales flying through the sky at any point if Miyazaki wanted and the world would be no less compelling for it. Miyazaki's stories are constantly full of unexplained phenomena: the bug-styled planes of *Castle in the Sky* which are inarguably inefficient and illogical but incredibly evocative. The hopping lantern in *Spirited Away* that serves as a point of hope in the dark.

Even if Miyazaki does have answers, he does not always give them to us, and none of these stories are worse off for it. These things just happen, and they add something to the world

---

[45] Nancy Kress "Ten Authors on the 'Hard' vs. 'Soft' Science Fiction Debate" (20 Feb 2017) Tor <www.tor.com>

on a different level—invoking a feeling, leaving an impression, altering the tone with regards to that psychological and emotional experience first. Allowing itself to be strange, to be unique, to be wholly outside the bounds of our usual rules without justification creates that enchanting feel that Ghibli films have, but it also means the world is adaptable enough to create settings and obstacles needed to tell the story however Miyazaki wants, rather than fitting a story to an established world. There is freedom in that.

Other soft worldbuilding stories include the *Dark Souls* game series, where the player is launched into a bizarre grimdark reality and left to puzzle it out on their own. HP Lovecraft and his imitators write stories dependent on that sense of the unknown and existential—these books almost *require* soft worldbuilding because having a totally explicable world would undermine the point of the psychological horror genre. These stories talk about humanity coming up against forces we cannot fathom or comprehend. It is an experiential world based in emotional and psychological reality, not an intellectual one. Jeff Vandermeer's *Annihilation* follows much the same pattern with a world defined by the inexplicable, united only by an experiential logic that we understand emotionally more than intellectually. Yoko Taro's *Nier* series employs similar strategies.

However, perhaps the most familiar soft-worldbuilt story is JK Rowling's *Harry Potter* series. Rowling has discussed how worldbuilding elements were added with each book—like the Department of Mysteries in *Harry Potter and the Order of the Phoenix* or the dementors in *Harry Potter and the Prisoner of Azkaban*—where they best support Harry's emotional arc. The world constantly grows and changes across the series, introducing elements that reflect the maturing tone of the series and the subject matter of each book.

Rowling did not waste time explaining how the currency worked or ensuring the currency even remotely made sense with seventeen sickles to a galleon, twenty-nine knuts in a sickle, and four-hundred-and-ninety-three knuts to a galleon. This bizarrely useless currency is just one small worldbuilding element used to show us how jovial and strange this world is compared to the mundane one. It may have little intellectual logic, but is wholly consistent with the experience Rowling wants to give the reader the feeling of being invited into this whimsical wizarding world. It is psychologically consistent with how wizards use owls for letters when they can teleport and let children wander forests at night for detention. Again, a different type of consistency.

Soft worldbuilt stories also excel at character-driven narratives. In Studio Ghibli's *Kiki's Delivery Service*, virtually nothing is communicated about how this world of witches and postal services works. Almost every town or city has its own witch with powers like foresight and flight, but worldbuilding elements are added in purely to support Kiki's arc. The story is all about how she wants to prove herself, works hard, burns out, and must learn to let herself rest. Almost nothing in Kiki's struggles come from her interacting with the worldbuilding around her. Little of the set-up and pay-off has anything to do with the worldbuilding, so not only can we spend the entirety of the story on that character journey, but the world at large does not need to justify itself. Pieces can be added where they support her arc without worrying about just how logical they are on their own.

JK Rowling captures that second strength in saying:

> 'Those characters belong to the readers as well as to me, and each has their own life in the heads of those who have read them. Sometimes the inner lives of characters as imagined by readers are not what I imagined for them, but the joy of books is that we all make our own mental cast.'[46]

---

[46] JK Rowling "Why Dumbledore went to the hilltop" (27 October 2015) Twitlonger <www.twitlonger.com>

This is true for both hard and soft worldbuilding, but where hard worldbuilding means we dictate to the reader what the world is like, soft worldbuilding invites them to give their input—making it an imaginative exercise as they read or watch. That is fun and immersive. For instance, cooperative tabletop games have used collaborative worldbuilding systems to create immersive experiences for decades.

Worldbuilding is not just about reader's understanding of the world; it is about crafting an atmosphere, tone, and mood, all of which contribute to immersion just as much, if not more, than detail. You can still create these things with hard worldbuilding, but it is a different method and usually has different results. Likewise, you can still create a grimdark world with soft worldbuilding, but that might come from a sensation of Lovecraftian powers bearing down on the characters rather than detailed knowledge of just how little food and water there is. This is the case in *Dark Souls*.

The crucial thing is this: while hard worldbuilding stories can absolutely have a lot of depth, the fewer requirements to rationalise soft worldbuilding choices means you can prioritise the meaning you want to imbue your world with.[47]

---

[47] This is, perhaps, why JK Rowling's 'clarifications' in recent years have fallen flat. The *Harry Potter* series is full of some of the most bizarre and incoherent worldbuilding I have ever seen from exchange rates to love potions being available to children, but the Wizarding World was not created to immerse readers through grounded detail and intricate consistent rules—spells, after all, are introduced from book to book to serve the story—but to immerse us through a feeling of whimsy and opportunity, and to also mirror the oddball characters, making it feel like the world and people fit together. All of this creates a light-hearted atmosphere that is slowly lost as the books go on and grow darker. But Rowling has, on occasion, tried to rationalise her soft worldbuilding, and it feels off. They feel like random conclusions we were never meant to reach, dispelling the magical atmosphere she originally had, and

Hard worldbuilding has taken the world by storm in recent decades, especially with the rise of the likes of GRR Martin and Brandon Sanderson and with Tolkien and Jordan at the genre's foundations. But that does not mean you should feel compelled to justify everything you create, especially things that are irrelevant to the set-up and pay-off in your story. Sometimes, things are bizarre, strange, or even nonsensical, and these can work to your advantage if they fit into those 'more profound things' for the reader. Crafting an atmosphere, vision, or experience first.

This is not to say that having incoherent and contradictory worldbuilding will work for you. Nothing guarantees your readers will see things the same way you do. If you want to try soft worldbuilding as an experiment, find a character-driven story you want to tell and figure out what lore is absolutely essential for the reader to understand about your world. Then build the rest of the world around them with those 'more profound' things in mind, using whatever strange or otherworldly imagery you like that fits the emotional logic you want to channel in your story.

Who knows?

You may even like it.

---

undermining the reader's involvement where they were originally invited to imagine.

Printed in Great Britain
by Amazon

38162015R00148